The Acadian Exiles: A Chronicle of the Land of Evangeline

by

Arthur G. Doughty

The Echo Library 2007

Published by

The Echo Library

Echo Library
131 High St.
Teddington
Middlesex TW11 8HH

www.echo-library.com

Please report serious faults in the text to
complaints@echo-library.com

ISBN 978-1-40682-577-0

CHAPTER I

THE FOUNDERS OF ACADIA

The name Acadia,[1] which we now associate with a great tragedy of history and song, was first used by the French to distinguish the eastern or maritime part of New France from the western part, which began with the St Lawrence valley and was called Canada. Just where Acadia ended and Canada began the French never clearly defined—in course of time, as will be seen, this question became a cause of war with the English—but we shall not be much at fault if we take a line from the mouth of the river Penobscot, due north to the St Lawrence, to mark the western frontier of the Acadia of the French. Thus, as the map shows, Acadia lay in that great peninsula which is flanked by two large islands, and is washed on the north and east by the river and gulf of St Lawrence, and on the south by the Atlantic Ocean; and it comprised what are to-day parts of Quebec and Maine, as well as the provinces of New Brunswick, Nova Scotia, and Prince Edward Island. When the French came, and for long after, this country was the hunting ground of tribes of the Algonquin race—Micmacs, Malecites, and Abnakis or Abenakis.

By right of the discoveries of Jean Verrazano (1524) and Jacques Cartier (1534-42) the French crown laid claim to all America north of the sphere of Spanish influence. Colonial enterprise, however, did not thrive during the religious wars which rent Europe in the sixteenth century; and it was not until after the Edict of Nantes in 1598 that France could follow up the discoveries of her seamen by an effort to colonize either

---

[1] The origin of the name is uncertain. By some authorities it is supposed to be derived from the Micmac algaty, signifying a camp or settlement. Others have traced it to the Micmac akade, meaning a place where something abounds. Thus, Sunakade (Shunacadie, C. B.), the cranberry place; Seguboon-akade (Shubenacadie), the place of the potato, etc. The earliest map marking the country, that of Ruscelli (1561), gives the name Lacardie. Andre Thivet, a French writer, mentions the country in 1575 as Arcadia; and many modern writers believe Acadia to be merely a corruption of that classic name.

Acadia or Canada. Abortive attempts had indeed been made by the Marquis de la Roche, but these had resulted only in the marooning of fifty unfortunate convicts on Sable Island. The first real colonizing venture of the French in the New World was that of the Sieur de Monts, the patron and associate of Champlain.[2] The site of this first colony was in Acadia. Armed with viceregal powers and a trading monopoly for ten years, De Monts gathered his colonists, equipped two ships, and set out from Havre de Grace in April 1604. The company numbered about a hundred and fifty Frenchmen of various ranks and conditions, from the lowest to the highest—convicts taken from the prisons, labourers and artisans, Huguenot ministers and Catholic priests, some gentlemen of noble birth, among them Jean de Biencourt, Baron de Poutrincourt, and the already famous explorer Champlain.

The vessels reached Cape La Heve on the south coast of Nova Scotia in May. They rounded Cape Sable, sailed up the Bay of Fundy, and entered the Annapolis Basin, which Champlain named Port Royal. The scene here so stirred the admiration of the Baron de Poutrincourt that he coveted the place as an estate for his family, and begged De Monts, who by his patent was lord of the entire country, to grant him the adjoining lands. De Monts consented; the estate was conveyed; and Poutrincourt became the seigneur of Port Royal.

The adventurers crossed to the New Brunswick shore, turned their vessel westward, passed the mouth of the river St John, which they named, and finally dropped anchor in Passamaquoddy Bay. Here, on a small island near the mouth of the river St Croix, now on the boundary-line between New Brunswick and Maine, De Monts landed his colonists. They cleared the ground; and, within an enclosure known as the Habitation de l'Isle Saincte-Croix, erected a few buildings—'one made with very fair and artificial carpentry work' for De Monts, while others, less ornamental, were for 'Monsieur d'Orville, Monsieur Champlein, Monsieur Champdore, and other men of high standing.'

---

[2] See The founder of New France in this Series, chap. ii.

Then as the season waned the vessels, which linked them to the world they had left, unfurled their sails and set out for France. Seventy-nine men remained at St Croix, among them De Monts and Champlain. In the vast solitude of forest they settled down for the winter, which was destined to be full of horrors. By spring thirty-five of the company had died of scurvy and twenty more were at the point of death. Evidently St Croix was not a good place for a colony. The soil was sandy and there was no fresh water. So, in June, after the arrival of a vessel bringing supplies from France, De Monts and Champlain set out to explore the coasts in search of a better site. But, finding none which they deemed suitable, they decided to tempt fortune at Poutrincourt's domain of Port Royal. Thither, then, in August the colonists moved, carrying their implements and stores across the Bay of Fundy, and landing on the north side of the Annapolis Basin, opposite Goat Island, where the village of Lower Granville now stands.

The colony thus formed at Port Royal in the summer of 1605—the first agricultural settlement of Europeans on soil which is now Canadian—had a broken existence of eight years. Owing to intrigues at the French court, De Monts lost his charter in 1607 and the colony was temporarily abandoned; but it was re-established in 1610 by Poutrincourt and his son Charles de Biencourt. The episode of Port Royal, one of the most lively in Canadian history, introduces to us some striking characters. Besides the leaders in the enterprise, already mentioned—De Monts, Champlain, Poutrincourt, and Biencourt—we meet here Lescarbot,[3] lawyer, merry philosopher, historian, and farmer; likewise, Louis Hebert, planting vines and sowing wheat—the same Louis Hebert who afterwards became the first tiller of the soil at Quebec. Here, also, is Membertou, sagamore of the Micmacs, 'a man of a hundred summers' and 'the most formidable savage within the memory of man.' Hither, too, in 1611, came the Jesuits Biard

---

[3] Lescarbot was the historian of the colony. His History of New France, reprinted by the Champlain Society (Toronto, 1911), with an English translation, notes, and appendices by W. L. Grant, is a delightful and instructive work.

and Masse, the first of the black-robed followers of Loyola to set foot in New France. But the colony was to perish in an event which foreshadowed the struggle in America between France and England. In 1613 the English Captain Argall from new-founded Virginia sailed up the coasts of Acadia looking for Frenchmen. The Jesuits had just begun on Mount Desert Island the mission of St Sauveur. This Argall raided and destroyed. He then went on and ravaged Port Royal. And its occupants, young Biencourt and a handful of companions, were forced to take to a wandering life among the Indians.

Twenty years passed before the French made another organized effort to colonize Acadia. The interval, however, was not without events which had a bearing on the later fortunes of the colony. Missionaries from Quebec, both Recollets and Jesuits, took up their abode among the Indians, on the river St John and at Nipisiguit on Chaleur Bay. Trading companies exploited the fur fields and the fisheries, and French vessels visited the coasts every summer. It was during this period that the English Puritans landed at Plymouth (1620), at Salem (1628), and at Boston (1630), and made a lodgment there on the south-west flank of Acadia. The period, too, saw Sir William Alexander's Scots in Nova Scotia and saw the English Kirkes raiding the settlements of New France.[4]

The Baron de Poutrincourt died in 1615, leaving his estate to his son Biencourt. And after Biencourt's own death in 1623, it was found that he had bequeathed a considerable fortune, including all his property and rights in Acadia, to his friend and companion, that interesting and resourceful adventurer, Charles de la Tour. This man, when a lad of fourteen, and his father, Claude de la Tour, had come out to Acadia in the service of Poutrincourt. After the destruction of Port Royal, Charles de la Tour had followed young Biencourt into the forest, and had lived with him the nomadic life of the Indians. Later, the elder La Tour established himself for trade at the mouth of the Penobscot, but he was driven away from this post by a party from the English colony at Plymouth. The younger La Tour, after coming into Biencourt's property, built Fort Lomeron,

---

[4] See The Jesuit Missions in this Series, chap. iv.

afterwards named St Louis, at the place now known as Port Latour, near Cape Sable. This made him in fact, if not in name, the French ruler of Acadia, for his Fort St Louis was the only place of any strength in the whole country.

By 1627 the survivors of Biencourt's wandering companions had settled down, some of them in their old quarters at Port Royal, but most of them with La Tour at Cape Sable. Then came to Acadia seventy Scottish settlers, sent hither by Sir William Alexander, who took up their quarters at Port Royal and named it Scots Fort. The French described these settlers as 'all kinds of vagabonds, barbarians, and savages from Scotland'; and the elder La Tour went to France to procure stores and ammunition, and to petition the king to grant his son a commission to hold Acadia against the intruders. But the elder La Tour was not to come back in the role of a loyal subject of France. He was returning in 1628 with the ships of the newly formed Company of One Hundred Associates, under Roquemont, when, off the Gaspe coast, appeared the hostile sail of the Kirkes; and La Tour was taken prisoner to England. There he entered into an alliance with the English, accepted grants of land from Sir William Alexander, had himself and his son made Baronets of Nova Scotia, and promised to bring his son over to the English side. Young La Tour, when his father returned, accepted the gift, and by some means procured also, in 1631, a commission from the French king as lieutenant-general of Acadia. Later, as we shall see, his dual allegiance proved convenient.

The restoration of Acadia to France in 1632, by the Treaty of St Germain-en-Laye, was to Cardinal Richelieu the signal for a renewal of the great colonizing project which he had set on foot five years earlier and which had been interrupted by the hostile activities of the Kirkes.[5] Richelieu appointed lieutenant-general of Acadia Isaac de Razilly, one of the Company of One Hundred Associates and commander of the Order of Malta, with authority to take over Acadia from the Scots. Razilly brought out with him three hundred settlers, recruited mainly

---

[5] See The founder of New France, chap. v, and The Jesuit Missions, chap. iv.

from the districts of Touraine and Brittany—the first considerable body of colonists to come to the country. He was a man of more than ordinary ability, of keen insight and affable manners. 'The commander,' wrote Champlain, 'possessed all the qualities of a good, a perfect sea-captain; prudent, wise, industrious; urged by the saintly motive of increasing the glory of God and of exercising his energy in New France in order to erect the cross of Christ and plant the lilies of France therein.' He planned for Acadia on a large scale. He endeavoured to persuade Louis XIII to maintain a fleet of twelve vessels for the service of the colony, and promised to bring out good settlers from year to year. Unfortunately, his death occurred in 1635 before his dreams could be realized. He had been given the power to name his successor; and on his death-bed he appointed his cousin and companion, Charles de Menou, Sieur d'Aulnay Charnisay, adjuring him 'not to abandon the country, but to pursue a task so gloriously begun.'

Years of strife and confusion followed. Razilly had made La Heve his headquarters; but Charnisay took up his at Port Royal.[6] This brought him into conflict with Charles de la Tour, who had now established himself at the mouth of the river St John, and whose commission from the king, giving him jurisdiction over the whole of Acadia, had, apparently, never been rescinded. The king, to whom the dispute was referred, instructed that an imaginary line should be drawn through the Bay of Fundy to divide the territory of Charnisay from that of La Tour. But this arrangement did not prevent the rivalry between the two feudal chiefs from developing into open warfare. In the struggle the honours rested with Charnisay. Having first undermined La Tour's influence at court, he attacked and captured La Tour's Fort St John. This happened in 1645. La Tour himself was absent; but his wife, a woman of

---

[6] Charnisay built his fort about six miles farther up than the original Port Royal, and on the opposite side of the river, at the place thenceforth known as Port Royal until 1710, and since then as Annapolis Royal or Annapolis.

heroic mould, made a most determined resistance.[7] La Tour was impoverished and driven into exile; his remarkable wife died soon afterwards; and Charnisay remained lord of all he surveyed. But Charnisay was not long to enjoy his dominion. In May 1650 he was thrown by accident from his canoe into the Annapolis river and died in consequence of the exposure.

In the year following Charnisay's death Charles de la Tour reappeared on the scene. Armed with a new patent from the French king, making him governor and lieutenant- general of Acadia, he took possession of his fort at the mouth of the St John, and further strengthened his position by marrying the widow of his old rival Charnisay. Three years later (1654), when the country fell again into the hands of the English, La Tour turned to good account his previous relations with them. He was permitted to retain his post, and lived happily with his wife[8] at Fort St John, so far as history records, until his death in 1666.

By the Treaty of Breda in 1667 Acadia was restored to France, and a period ensued of unbroken French rule. The history of the forty-three years from the Treaty of Breda until the English finally took possession is first a history of slow but peaceful development, and latterly of raids and bloody strife in which French and English and Indians were involved. In 1671 the population, according to a census of that year, numbered less than four hundred and fifty. This was presently increased by sixty new colonists from France. By 1685 this population had more than doubled and the tiny settlements appeared to be thriving. But after 1690 war again racked the land.

During this period Acadia was under the government of Quebec, but there was always a local governor. The first of these, Hubert de Grandfontaine, came out in 1670. He and some of his successors were men of force and ability; but

---

[7] This follows the story as told by Denys (see p. 18 note), which has been generally accepted by historians. But Charnisay in an elaborate memoir (Memoire Instructif) gives a very different version of this affair.

[8] They had five children, who married and settled in Acadia. Many of their descendants may be counted among the Acadian families living at the present time in Nova Scotia and New Brunswick.

others, such as Brouillan, who issued card money without authority and applied torture to an unconvicted soldier, and Perrot, who sold liquor by the pint and the half-pint in his own house, were unworthy representatives of the crown.

By 1710 the population of Acadia had grown to about twenty-one hundred souls, distributed chiefly in the districts of Port Royal, Minas, and Chignecto. Most of these were descended from the settlers brought over by Razilly and Charnisay between 1633 and 1638. On the whole, they were a strong, healthy, virtuous people, sincerely attached to their religion and their traditions. The most notable singularity of their race was stubbornness, although they could be led by kindness where they could not be driven by force. Though inclined to litigation, they were not unwilling to arbitrate their differences. They 'had none who were bred mechanics; every farmer was his own architect and every man of property a farmer.' 'The term Mister was unknown among them.' They took pride in their appearance and wore most attractive costumes, in which black and red colours predominated. Content with the product of their labour and having few wants, they lived in perfect equality and with extreme frugality. In an age when learning was confined to the few, they were not more illiterate than the corresponding class in other countries. 'In the summer the men were continually employed in husbandry.' They cultivated chiefly the rich marsh-lands by the rivers and the sea, building dikes along the banks and shores to shut out the tides; and made little effort to clear the woodlands. 'In the winter they were engaged in cutting timber and wood for fuel and fencing, and in hunting; the women in carding, spinning, and weaving wool, flax, and hemp, of which their country furnished abundance; these, with furs from bears, beavers, foxes, otters, and martens, gave them not only comfortable, but in some cases handsome clothing.' Although they had large herds of cattle, 'they never made any merchantable butter, being used to set their milk in small noggins which were kept in such order as to turn it thick and sour in a short time, of which they ate voraciously.'[9]

---

[9] Public Archives, Canada, Brown Collection, M 651a, 171.

The lands which the Acadians reclaimed from the sea and cultivated were fertile in the extreme. A description has come down to us of what was doubtless a typical Acadian garden. In it were quantities of 'very fine well-headed cabbages and of all other sorts of pot herbs and vegetables.' Apple and pear trees brought from France flourished. The peas were 'so covered with pods that it could only be believed by seeing.' The wheat was particularly good. We read of one piece of land where 'each grain had produced six or eight stems, and the smallest ear was half a foot in length, filled with grain.' The streams and rivers, too, teemed with fish. The noise of salmon sporting in the rivers sounded like the rush of a turbulent rapid, and a catch such as 'ten men could not haul to land' was often made in a night. Pigeons were a plague, alighting in vast flocks in the newly planted gardens. If the economic progress of the country had been slow, the reason had lain, not in any poverty of natural resources, but in the scantiness of the population, the neglect of the home government, the incessant turmoil within, and the devastating raids of English enemies.

CHAPTER II

THE BRITISH IN ACADIA

Almost from the first England had advanced claims, slender though they were, to the ownership of Acadia. And very early, as we have seen, the colony had been subjected to the scourge of English attacks.

Argall's expedition had been little more than a buccaneering exploit and an earnest of what was to come. Nor did any permanent result, other than the substitution of the name Nova Scotia for Acadia, flow from Sir William Alexander's enterprise. Alexander, afterwards Lord Stirling, was a Scottish courtier in the entourage of James I, from whom he obtained in 1621 a grant of the province of New Scotland or Nova Scotia. A year later he sent out a small body of farm hands and one artisan, a blacksmith, to establish a colony. The expedition miscarried; and another in the next year shared a similar fate. A larger company of Scots, however, as already mentioned, settled at Port Royal in 1627 and erected a fort, known as Scots Fort, on the site of the original settlement of De Monts. This colony, with some reinforcements from Scotland, stood its ground until the country was ceded to France in 1632. On the arrival of Razilly in that year most of the Scottish settlers went home, and the few who remained were soon merged in the French population.

For twenty-two years after this Acadia remained French, under the feudal sway of its overlords, Razilly, Charnisay, La Tour, and Nicolas Denys, the historian of Acadia.[10] But in 1654 the fleet of Robert Sedgwick suddenly appeared off Port Royal and compelled its surrender in the name of Oliver Cromwell. Then for thirteen years Acadia was nominally English. Sir Thomas Temple, the governor during this period, tried to induce English-speaking people to settle in the province, but with small success. England's hold of Acadia was,

[10] He wrote The Description and Natural History of the Coasts of North America. An edition, translated and edited, with a memoir of the author, by W. F. Ganong, will be found in the publications of the Champlain Society (Toronto, 1908).

in fact, not very firm. The son of Emmanuel Le Borgne, who claimed the whole country by right of a judgment he had obtained in the French courts against Charnisay, apparently found little difficulty in turning the English garrison out of the fort at La Heve, leaving his unfortunate victims without means of return to New England, or of subsistence; but in such destitution that they were forced 'to live upon grass and to wade in the water for lobsters to keep them alive.' Some amusing correspondence followed between France and England. The French ambassador in London complained of the depredations committed in the house of a certain Monsieur de la Heve. The English government, better informed about Acadia, replied that it knew of no violence committed in the house of M. de la Heve. 'Neither is there any such man in the land, but there is a place so called, which Temple purchased for eight thousand pounds from La Tour, where he built a house. But one M. le Borny, two or three years since, by force took it, so that the violence was on Le Borny's part.' The strife was ended, however, as already mentioned, by the Treaty of Breda in 1667, in the return of Acadia to France in exchange for the islands in the West Indies of St Christopher, Antigua, and Montserrat.

Nearly a quarter of a century passed. France and England were at peace and Acadia enjoyed freedom from foreign attack. But the accession of William of Orange to the throne of England heralded the outbreak of another Anglo-French war. The month of May 1690 saw Sir William Phips with a New England fleet and an army of over a thousand men off Port Royal, demanding its surrender. Menneval, the French governor, yielded his fortress on the understanding that he and the garrison should be transported to French soil. Phips, however, after pillaging the place, desecrating the church, hoisting the English flag, and obliging the inhabitants to take the oath of allegiance to William and Mary, carried off his prisoners to Boston. He was bent on the capture of Quebec in the same year and had no mind to make the necessary arrangements to hold Acadia. Hardly had he departed when a relief expedition from France, under the command of Menneval's brother Villebon, sailed into Port Royal. But as

Villebon had no sufficient force to reoccupy the fort, he pulled down the English flag, replaced it by that of France, and proceeded to the river St John. After a conference with the Indians there he went to Quebec, and was present with Frontenac in October when Phips appeared with his summons to surrender.[11] Villebon then went to France. A year later he returned as governor of Acadia and took up his quarters at Fort Jemseg, about fifty miles up the St John river. Here he organized war-parties of Indians to harry the English settlements; and the struggle continued, with raid and counter-raid, until 1697, when the Treaty of Ryswick halted the war between the two crowns.

The formal peace, however, was not for long. In 1702 Queen Anne declared war against France and Spain. And before peace returned the final capture of Acadia had been effected. It was no fault of Subercase, the French officer who in 1706 came to Port Royal as governor, that the fortunes of war went against him. In 1707 he beat off two violent attacks of the English; and if sufficient means had been placed at his disposal, he might have retained the colony for France. But the ministry at Versailles, pressed on all sides, had no money to spare for the succour of Acadia. Subercase set forth with clearness the resources of the colony, and urged strong reasons in favour of its development. In 1708 a hundred soldiers came to his aid; but as no funds for their maintenance came with them, they became a burden. The garrison was reduced almost to starvation; and Subercase was forced to replenish his stores by the capture of pirate vessels. The last letter he wrote home was filled with anguish over the impending fate of Port Royal. His despair was not without cause. In the spring of 1710 Queen Anne placed Colonel Francis Nicholson, one of her leading colonial officers, in command of the troops intended for the recovery of Nova Scotia. An army of about fifteen hundred soldiers was raised in New England, and a British fleet gathered in Boston Harbour. On October 5 (New Style) this expedition arrived before Port Royal. The troops landed and laid siege once more to the much-harassed capital of Acadia. The result

---

[11] See The Fighting Governor in this Series, chap. vii.

was a foregone conclusion. Five days later preliminary proposals were exchanged between Nicholson and Subercase. The starving inhabitants petitioned Subercase to give up. He held out, however, till the cannonade of the enemy told him that he must soon yield to force. He then sent an officer to Nicholson to propose the terms of capitulation. It was agreed that the garrison should march out with the honours of war and be transported to France in English ships, and that the inhabitants within three miles of the fort should 'remain upon their estates, with their corn, cattle, and furniture, during two years, in case they are not desirous to go before, they taking the oath of allegiance and fidelity to Her Sacred Majesty of Great Britain.' Then to the roll of the drum, and with all the honours of war, the French troops marched out and the New Englanders marched in. The British flag was raised, and, in honour of the queen of England, Port Royal was named Annapolis Royal. A banquet was held in the fortress to celebrate the event, and the French officers and their ladies were invited to it to drink the health of Queen Anne, while cannon on the bastions and cannon on the ramparts thundered forth a royal salute.

The celebration over, Subercase sent an envoy to Quebec, to inform Vaudreuil, the governor of New France, of the fall of Port Royal, and then embarked with his soldiers for France. A few days later Nicholson took away most of his troops and repaired to Boston, leaving a garrison of four hundred and fifty men and officers under the command of Colonel Samuel Vetch to hold the newly-won post until peace should return and Her Majesty's pleasure concerning it be made known.

As far as he was able, Vetch set up military rule at Annapolis Royal. He administered the oath of allegiance to the inhabitants of the banlieue—within three miles of the fort— according to the capitulation, and established a court to try their disputes. Many and grave difficulties faced the new governor and his officers. The Indians were hostile, and, quite naturally in the state of war which prevailed, emissaries of the French strove to keep the Acadians unfriendly to their English masters. Moreover, Vetch was badly in want of money. The soldiers had no proper clothing for the winter; they had not been paid for their services; the fort stood in need of repair; and the military chest was empty. He could get no assistance from Boston or London, and his only resource seemed to be to levy on the inhabitants in the old-fashioned way of conquerors. The Acadians pleaded poverty, but Vetch sent out armed men to enforce his order, and succeeded in collecting at least a part of the tribute he demanded, not only from the inhabitants round the fort over whom he had authority, but also from the settlers of Minas and Chignecto, who were not included in the capitulation.

The first winter passed, in some discomfort and privation, but without any serious mishap to the English soldiers. With the month of June, however, there came a disaster. The Acadians had been directed to cut timber for the repair of the fort and deliver it at Annapolis. They had complied for a time and had then quit work, fearing, as they said, attacks from the Indian allies of the French, who threatened to kill them if they aided the enemy. Thereupon Vetch ordered an officer to take seventy-five men and go up the river to the place where the timber was being felled and 'inform the people that if they would bring it down they would receive every imaginable protection,' but if they were averse or delayed to do so he was to 'threaten them with severity.' 'And let the soldiers make a show of killing their hogs,' the order ran, 'but do not kill any, and let them kill some fowls, but pay for them before you come away.' Armed with this somewhat peculiar military order, the troops set out. But as they ascended the river they were waylaid by a war-party of French and Indians, and within an hour every man of the seventy-five English was either killed or taken captive.

Soon after this tragic affair Vetch went to Boston to take a hand in an invasion of Canada which was planned for that summer. This invasion was to take place by both sea and land simultaneously. Vetch joined the fleet of Sir Hovenden Walker, consisting of some sixty vessels which sailed from Boston in July. Meanwhile Colonel Nicholson stood near Lake Champlain, with a force of several thousand colonial troops and Six Nation Indians, in readiness to advance on Canada to co-operate with the fleet. But the fleet never got within striking distance. Not far above the island of Anticosti some of the ships ran aground and were wrecked with a loss of nearly a thousand men; and the commander gave up the undertaking and bore away for England. When news of this mishap reached Nicholson he retreated and disbanded his men. But, though the ambitious enterprise ended ingloriously, it was not wholly fruitless, for it kept the French of Quebec on guard at home; while but for this menace they would probably have sent a war-party in force to drive the English out of Acadia.

The situation of the English at Annapolis was indeed critical. Their numbers had been greatly reduced by disease and raids and the men were in a sorry plight for lack of provisions and clothing. Vetch could obtain neither men nor money from England or the colonies. Help, however, of a sort did come in the summer of 1712. This was in the form of a band of Six Nation Indians, allies of the English, from the colony of New York.[12] These savages pitched their habitations not far from the fort, and thereafter the garrison suffered less from the Micmac and Abnaki allies of the French.

The Acadians were in revolt; and as long as they cherished the belief that their countrymen would recover Acadia, all attempts to secure their allegiance to Queen Anne proved unavailing. At length, in April 1713, the Treaty of Utrecht set at rest the question of the ownership of the country. Cape Breton, Ile St Jean (Prince Edward Island), and other islands in the Gulf were left in the hands of the French. But Newfoundland and 'all Nova Scotia or Acadia, with its ancient boundaries, as also the city of Port Royal, now called Annapolis Royal,' passed to the British crown.

---

[12] Collections of the Nova Scotia Historical Society, vol. iv, p. 41.

CHAPTER III

THE OATH OF ALLEGIANCE

We have now to follow a sequence of events leading up to the calamity to be narrated in a later chapter. By the Treaty of Utrecht the old king, Louis XIV, had obtained certain guarantees for his subjects in Acadia. It was provided that 'they may have liberty to remove themselves within a year to any other place with all their movable effects'; and that 'those who are willing to remain therein and to be subject to the kingdom of Britain are to enjoy the free exercise of their religion.' And these terms were confirmed by a warrant of Queen Anne addressed to Nicholson, under date of June 23, 1713.[13] The status of the Acadians under the treaty, reinforced by this warrant, seems to be sufficiently clear. If they wished to become British subjects, which of course implied taking the oath of allegiance, they were to enjoy all the privileges of citizenship, not accorded at that time to Catholics in Great Britain, as well as the free exercise of their religion. But if they preferred to remove to another country within a year, they were to have that liberty.

---

[13] 'Trusty and Well-beloved, We greet you Well! Whereas Our Good Brother the Most Christian King hath at Our desire released from imprisonment on board His Galleys, such of His subjects as were detained there on account of their professing the Protestant religion, We being willing to show by some mark of Our Favour towards His subjects how kindly we take His compliance therein, have therefore thought fit hereby to Signifie Our Will and Pleasure to you that you permit and allow such of them as have any lands or Tenements in the Places under your Government in Acadie and Newfoundland, that have been or are to be yielded to Us by Vertue of the late Treaty of Peace, and are Willing to Continue our Subjects to retain and Enjoy their said Lands and Tenements without any Lett or Molestation as fully and freely as other our Subjects do or may possess their Lands and Estates or to sell the same if they shall rather Chuse to remove elsewhere—And for so doing this shall be your Warrant, And so we bid you fare well. Given at our Court at Kensington the 23rd day of June 1713 in the Twelfth Year of our Reign.'—Public Archives, Canada. Nova Scotia A, vol. iv, p. 97.

The French authorities were not slow to take advantage of this part of the treaty. In order to hold her position in the New World and assert her authority, France had transferred the garrison which she had formerly maintained at Placentia, Newfoundland, to Cape Breton. This island she had renamed Ile Royale, and here she was shortly to rear the great fortress of Louisbourg. It was to her interest to induce the Acadians to remove to this new centre of French influence. In March 1713, therefore, the French king intimated his wish that the Acadians should emigrate to Ile Royale; every inducement, indeed, must be offered them to settle there; though he cautioned his officers that if any of the Acadians had already taken the oath of allegiance to Great Britain, great care must be exercised to avoid scandal.

Many Acadians, then, on receiving attractive offers of land in Ile Royale, applied to the English authorities for permission to depart. The permission was not granted. It was first refused by Governor Vetch on the ground that he was retiring from office and was acting only in the absence of Colonel Nicholson, who had been recently appointed governor. The truth is that the English regarded with alarm the removal of practically the entire population from Nova Scotia. The governor of Ile Royale intervened, and sent agents to Annapolis Royal to make a formal demand on behalf of the Acadians, presenting in support of his demand the warrant of Queen Anne. The inhabitants, it was said, wished to leave Nova Scotia and settle in Ile Royale, and 'they expect ships to convey themselves and effects accordingly.' Nicholson, who had now arrived as governor, took the position that he must refer the question to England for the consideration of Her Majesty.

When the demand of the governor of Ile Royale reached England, Vetch was in London; and Vetch had financial interests in Nova Scotia. He at once appealed to the Lords of Trade, who in due course protested to the sovereign 'that this would strip Nova Scotia and greatly strengthen Cape Breton.' Time passed, however, and the government made no pronouncement on the question. Meanwhile Queen Anne had died. Matters drifted. The Acadians wished to leave, but were not allowed to employ British vessels. In despair they began to construct small boats on their own account, to carry their families and effects to Ile Royale. These boats, however, were seized by order of Nicholson, and the Acadians were explicitly forbidden to remove or to dispose of their possessions until a decision with regard to the question should arrive from England.

In January 1715 the accession of George I was proclaimed throughout Acadia. But when the Acadians were required to swear allegiance to the new monarch, they proved obdurate. They agreed not to do anything against His Britannic Majesty as long as they remained in Acadia; but they refused to take the oath on the plea that they had already pledged their word to migrate to Ile Royale. John Doucette, who arrived in the colony in October 1717 as lieutenant-governor, was informed by the Acadians that 'the French inhabitants had never own'd His Majesty as Possessor of this His Continent of Nova Scotia and L'Acadie.' When Doucette presented a paper for them to sign, promising them the same protection and liberty as the rest of His Majesty's subjects in Acadia, they brought forward a document of their own, which evidently bore the marks of honest toil, since Doucette 'would have been glad to have sent' it to the secretary of state 'in a cleaner manner.' In it they declared, 'We shall be ready to carry into effect the demand proposed to us, as soon as His Majesty shall have done us the favour of providing some means of sheltering us from the savage tribes, who are always ready to do all kinds of mischief... In case other means cannot be found, we are ready to take an oath, that we will take up arms neither against His Britannic Majesty, nor against France, nor against any of their subjects or allies.'[14]

The attitude of both France and England towards the unfortunate Acadians was thoroughly selfish. The French at Louisbourg, after their first attempt to bring the Acadians to Ile Royale, relapsed into inaction. They still hoped doubtless that Acadia would be restored to France, and while they would have been glad to welcome the Acadians, they perceived the advantage of keeping them under French influence in British

[14] Public Archives, Canada. Nova Scotia A, vol. viii, p. 181 et seq.

territory. In order to do this they had at their hand convenient means. The guarantee to the Acadians of the freedom of their religion had entailed the presence in Acadia of French priests not British subjects, who were paid by the French government and were under the direction of the bishop of Quebec. These priests were, of course, loyal to France and inimical to Great Britain. Another source of influence possessed by the French lay in their alliance with the Indian tribes, an alliance which the missionary priests helped to hold firm. The fear of an Indian attack was destined on more than one occasion to keep the Acadians loyal to France. On the other hand, the British, while loth to let the Acadians depart, did little to improve their lot. It was a period of great economy in English colonial administration. Walpole, in his desire to reduce taxation, devoted very little money to colonial development; and funds were doled out to the authorities at Annapolis in the most parsimonious manner. 'It is a pity,' wrote Newton, the collector of the customs at Annapolis and Canso, in 1719, that 'so fine a province as Nova Scotia should lie so long neglected. As for furs, feathers, and a fishery, we may challenge any province in America to produce the like, and beside that here is a good grainery; masting and naval stores might be provided hence. And was here a good establishment fixt our returns would be very advantageous to the Crown and Great Britain.' As it was, the British ministers were content to send out elaborate instructions for the preservation of forests, the encouragement of fisheries and the prevention of foreign trade, without providing either means for carrying out the schemes, or troops for the protection of the country.

Nothing further was done regarding the oath of allegiance until the arrival of Governor Philipps in 1720, when the Acadians were called upon to take the oath or leave the country within four months, taking with them only two sheep per family. This, it seems, was merely an attempt to intimidate the people into taking the oath, for when the Acadians, having no boats at their disposal, proposed to travel by land, and began to cut out a road for the passage of vehicles, they were stopped in the midst of their labours by order of the governor.

In a letter to England Philipps expressed the opinion that the Acadians, if left alone, would no doubt become contented British subjects, that their emigration at this time would be a distinct loss to the garrison, which was supplied by their labours. He added that the French were active in maintaining their influence over them. One potent factor in keeping them restless was the circulation of reports that the English would not much longer tolerate Catholicism.[15] The Lords of Trade took this letter into consideration, and in their reply of December 28, 1720, we find the proposal to remove the Acadians as a means of settling the problem.[16] This, however, was not the first mooting of the idea. During the same year Paul Mascarene, in 'A Description of Nova Scotia,' had given two reasons for the expulsion of the inhabitants: first, that they were Roman Catholics, under the full control of French priests opposed to British interests; secondly, that they continually incited the Indians to do mischief or disturb English settlements. On the other hand, Mascarene discovered two motives for retaining them: first, in order that they might not strengthen the French establishments; secondly, that they might be employed in furnishing supplies for the garrison and in

---

[15] Public Archives, Canada. Nova Scotia A, vol. xi, p. 186.

[16] 'As to the French inhabitants of Nova Scotia, who appear so wavering in their inclinations, we are apprehensive they will never become good subjects to His Majesty whilst the French Governors and their Priests retain so great an influence over them, for which reason we are of opinion, that they ought to be removed so soon as the forces which we have proposed to be sent to you shall arrive in Nova Scotia for the protection and better settlement of your Province, but as you are not to attempt their removal without His Majesty's positive orders for that purpose, you will do well in the meanwhile to continue the same prudent and cautious conduct towards them, to endeavour to undeceive them concerning the exercise of their religion, which will doubtless be allowed them if it should be thought proper to let them stay where they are.'—Public Archives, Canada. Nova Scotia A, vol. xii, p. 210.

preparing fortifications until such time as the English were strong enough to do without them.[17]

It does not appear that either the English or the French government had any paternal affection for the poor Acadians; but each was fully conscious of the use to which they might be put.

In a letter to the Lords of Trade Philipps sums up the situation. 'The Acadians,' he says, 'decline to take the oath of allegiance on two grounds—that in General Nicholson's time they had signed an obligation to continue subjects of France and retire to Cape Breton, and that the Indians would cut their throats if they became Englishmen.'

If they are permitted [he continues] to remain upon the footing they propose, it is very probable they will be obedient to government as long as the two Crowns continue in alliance, but in case of a rupture will be so many enemies in our bosom, and I cannot see any hopes, or likelihood, of making them English, unless it was possible to procure these Priests to be recalled who are tooth and nail against the Regent; not sticking to say openly that it is his day now, but will be theirs anon; and having others sent in their stead, which (if anything) may contribute in a little time to make some change in their sentiments.

He further suggests an 'oath of obliging the Acadians to live peaceably,' to take up arms against the Indians, but not against the French, to acknowledge the king's right to the country, to obey the government, and to hold their lands of the king by a new tenure, 'instead of holding them (as at present) from lords of manors who are now at Cape Breton, where at this day they pay their rent.'[18]

---

[17] 'A Description of Nova Scotia,' by Paul Mascarene, transmitted to the Lords of Trade by Governor Philipps.—Public Archives, Canada. Nova Scotia A, vol. xii, p. 118.

[18] Public Archives, Canada. Nova Scotia A, vol. xii, p. 96.

There were signs that the situation was not entirely hopeless. The Acadians were not allowed to leave the country, or even to settle down to the enjoyment of their homes; they were employed in supplying the needs of the troops, or in strengthening the British fortifications; yet they seem to have patiently accepted the inevitable. The Indians committed acts of violence, but the Acadians remained peaceable. There was, too, a certain amount of intermarriage between Acadian girls and the British soldiers. In those early days of Nova Scotia, girls of a marriageable age were few and were much sought after. There was in Annapolis an old French gentlewoman 'whose daughters, granddaughters, and other relatives' had married British officers. These ladies soon acquired considerable influence and were allowed to do much as they pleased. The old gentlewoman, Marie Magdalen Maisonat, who had married Mr William Winniett, a leading merchant and one of the first British inhabitants of Annapolis, became all-powerful in the town, not only on account of her own estimable qualities, but also on account of the position held by her daughters and granddaughters. Soldiers arrested for breach of discipline often pleaded that they had been 'sent for to finish a job of work for Madame'; and this excuse was usually sufficient to secure an acquittal. If not, the old lady would on her own authority order the culprit's release, and 'no further enquiry was made into the matter.' One British officer, who had incurred her displeasure, was told that 'Me have rendered King Shorge more important service dan ever you did or peut-etre ever shall, and dis is well known to peoples en autorite,' which may have been true if, as was asserted, she sometimes presided at councils of war in the fort.[19]

It was with the Indians, rather than with the Acadians, that the authorities had the greatest trouble. After several hostile acts had been committed, the governor determined to try the effect of the gentle art of persuasion. He sent to England an agent named Bannfield to purchase a large quantity of presents

---

[19] Knox, An Historical Journal of the Campaigns in North America, Edited, etc., by A. G. Doughty. Vol. i, pp. 94-6. (Toronto: The Champlain Society, 1914.)

for the Indians. Bannfield was thoroughly dishonest, and appropriated two-thirds of the money to his own use, expending the remainder on the purchase of articles of 'exceeding bad quality.' A gorgeous entertainment was prepared for the savages, and the presents were given to them. The Indians took away the presents, but their missionaries had little difficulty in showing them the inferiority of the English gifts; and Philipps noted that they did not appear satisfied. 'They will take all we give them,' he wrote, 'and cut our throats next day.' At length the Indians boldly declared war against the British, an action which Philipps attributed to the scandalous conduct of the agent Bannfield. At the instigation of the French of Ile Royale, they kept up hostilities for two years and committed many barbarities. The Micmacs seized fishing smacks, and killed and scalped a number of English soldiers and fishermen. It was not until a more attractive supply of presents arrived, and were distributed among the chiefs, that they could be induced to make peace.

During the progress of the Indian war Governor Philipps had prudently refrained from discussing with the Acadians the question of the oath; but in 1726 Lawrence Armstrong, the lieutenant-governor, resolved to take up the matter again. In the district of Annapolis he had little trouble. The inhabitants there consented, after some discussion, to sign a declaration of allegiance, with a clause exempting them from the obligation of taking up arms.[20] But to deal with the Acadians of Minas and of Beaubassin on Chignecto Bay proved more difficult. Certain 'anti-monarchical traders' from Boston and evil-intentioned French inhabitants had represented in these districts that the governor had no authority in the land, and no power to administer oaths. No oath would these Acadians take but to their own Bon Roy de France. They promised, however, to pay all the rights and dues which the British demanded.

The death of George I in 1727, and the accession of George II, made it necessary for the Acadians to acknowledge the new monarch. This time the lieutenant-governor was

[20] This oath applied only to the inhabitants of the district of Annapolis.

determined to do the business in a thorough and comprehensive manner. He chartered a vessel at a cost of a hundred pounds, and commissioned Ensign Wroth to proceed from place to place at the head of a detachment of troops proclaiming the new king and obtaining the submission of the people. Wroth was eminently successful in proclaiming His Majesty; but he had less success in regard to the oath. Finding the Acadians obdurate, he promised them on his own authority freedom in the exercise of their religion, exemption from bearing arms, and liberty to withdraw from the province at any time. These 'unwarrantable concessions' Armstrong refused to ratify; and the Council immediately declared them null and void, although they resolved that 'the inhabitants...having signed and proclaimed His Majesty and thereby acknowledged his title and authority to and over this Province, shall have the liberties and privileges of English subjects.'[21] This was all the Acadians wished for.

The commission of Ensign Wroth did not extend to the district of Annapolis, which was dealt with by the Council. The deputies of the Acadians there were summoned to appear before the Council on September 6, 1727. But the inhabitants, instead of answering the summons, called a meeting on their own account and passed a resolution, signed by seventy-one of their people, which they forwarded to the Council. In this document they offered to take the oath on the conditions offered by Wroth. This the Council considered 'insolent and defiant,' and ordered the arrest of the deputies. On September 16 Charles Landry, Guillaume Bourgois, Abraham Bourg, and Francois Richard were brought before the Council, and, on refusing to take the oath except on the terms proposed by themselves, were committed to prison for contempt and disrespect to His Majesty. Next day the lieutenant-governor announced that 'they had been guilty of several enormous crimes in assembling the inhabitants in a riotous manner contrary to the orders of government both as to time and place and likewise in framing a rebellious paper.' It was then resolved: 'That Charles Landry, Guillaume Bourgois and Francis Richard,

---

[21] Public Archives, Canada. Nova Scotia B, vol. i, p. 177.

for their said offence, and likewise for refusing the oath of fidelity to His Majesty which was duly tendered them, be remanded to prison, laid in irons, and there remain until His Majesty's pleasure shall be made known concerning them, and that Abraham Bourg, in consideration of his great age, shall have leave to retire out of this His Majesty's Province, according to his desire and promise, by the first opportunity, leaving his effects behind him.'[22] The rest of the inhabitants were to be debarred from fishing on the British coasts. It is difficult to reconcile the actions of the Council. The inhabitants who cheerfully subscribed to the oath, with the exceptions made by Ensign Wroth, were to be accorded the privileges of British subjects, while some of those who would have been glad to accept the same terms were laid in irons, and the others debarred from fishing, their main support.

Shortly after this Philipps was compelled to return to Nova Scotia in order to restore tranquillity; for his lieutenant Armstrong, a man of quick temper, had fallen foul of the French priests, especially the Abbe Breslay, whom he had caused to be handled somewhat roughly. Armstrong, seeking an alliance with the Abnakis, had been foiled by the French and had laid the blame at the door of the priest, demanding the keys of the church and causing the presbytery to be pillaged. In the end Breslay had escaped in fear of his life. It was his complaints, set forth in a memorial to the government, that had brought about Philipps's return. The Acadians, with whom Philipps was popular, welcomed him in a public manner; and Philipps took advantage of the occasion to approach them again on the subject of the oath. He restored the Abbe Breslay to his flock, promised the people freedom in religious matters, and assured them that they would not be required to take up arms. Then all the Acadians in the district of Annapolis subscribed to the following oath: 'I promise and swear on the faith of a Christian that I will be truly faithful and will submit myself to His Majesty King George the Second, whom I acknowledge as the lord and sovereign of Nova Scotia or Acadia. So help me God.' In the spring of 1728 Philipps

---

[22] Public Archives, Canada. Nova Scotia B, vol. i, p. 159.

obtained also the submission of the inhabitants of the other districts, on similar terms; and even the Indians professed a willingness to submit. This was a triumph for the administration of Philipps, and laid at rest for a time the vexed question of the oath. The triumph was, however, more superficial than real, as we shall see by and by.

CHAPTER IV

IN TIMES OF WAR

When Philipps had set at rest the question of the oath of allegiance, he returned to England, and Armstrong, less pacific than his chief, again assumed the administration, and again had some trouble with the priests. Two Acadian missionaries had been expelled from the country for want of respect to the governor; and Armstrong informed the inhabitants that in future he must be consulted regarding the appointment of ecclesiastics, and that men from Quebec would not be acceptable. Brouillan, the governor of Ile Royale, had taken the ground that the Acadian priests, not being subjects of Great Britain, were not amenable to the British authorities. This view was held by the priests themselves. The president of the Navy Board at Paris, however, rebuked Brouillan, and informed him that the priests in Acadia should by word and example teach the obedience due to His Britannic Majesty. This pronouncement cleared the air; the disagreements with the missionaries were soon adjusted; and one of them, St Poncy, after being warned to cultivate the goodwill of the governor, was permitted to resume his pastoral duties at Annapolis Royal.

On the death of Armstrong, on December 6, 1739, from wounds supposed to have been inflicted by his own hand, John Adams was appointed lieutenant-governor and president of the Council. In the following spring, however, Adams was displaced by a vote of the Council in favour of Major Paul Mascarene. 'The Secretary came to my House,' wrote Adams to the Duke of Newcastle, 'and reported to me the judgment of the Council in favour of Major Mascarene, from whose judgment I appealed to His Majesty and said if you have done well by the House of Jerubable [Jerubbaal] then rejoice ye in Abimelech and let Abimelech rejoice in you.'[23] After this lucid appeal, Adams, who had deep religious convictions, retired to Boston and bemoaned the unrighteousness of Annapolis.[24]

---

[23] Public Archives, Canada. Nova Scotia A, vol. xxv, p. 9.
[24] Writing from Boston to the Lords of Trade, Adams said: 'I would have returned to Annapolis before now. But there was no Chaplain in

It was under Mascarene's administration that Nova Scotia passed through the period of warfare which now supervened. For some time relations between France and England had been growing strained in the New World, owing chiefly to the fact that the Peace of Utrecht had left unsettled the perilous question of boundary between the rival powers. There was the greatest confusion as to the boundaries of Nova Scotia or Acadia. The treaty had given Great Britain the province of Acadia 'with its ancient boundaries.' The 'ancient boundaries,' Great Britain claimed, included the whole mainland of the present maritime provinces and the Gaspe peninsula; whereas France contended that they embraced only the peninsula of Nova Scotia. Both powers, therefore, claimed the country north of the isthmus of Chignecto, and the definition of the boundary became a more and more pressing question.

The outbreak of the war of the Austrian Succession in Europe in 1741 set the match to the fuse. By 1744 the French and English on the Atlantic seaboard were up in arms. The governor of Ile Royale lost no time in attacking Nova Scotia. He invaded the settlements at Canso with about five hundred men; and presently a band of Indians, apparently led by the Abbe Le Loutre, missionary to the Micmacs, marched against Annapolis Royal. Towards these aggressions the Acadians assumed an attitude of strict neutrality. On the approach of Le Loutre's Micmacs they went to their homes, refusing to take part in the affair. Then when the raiders withdrew, on the arrival of reinforcements from Boston, the Acadians returned to their work on the fort. During the same year, when Du Vivier with a considerable French force appeared before Annapolis, the Acadians aided him with provisions. But when

---

the Garrison to administer God's word and sacrament to the people. But the Officers and Soldiers in Garrison have Prophaned the Holy Sacrament of Baptism and Ministeriall Function, by presuming to Baptize their own children. Why His Majesty's Chaplain does not come to his Duty I know not, but am persuaded it is a Disservice and Dishonour to our Religion and Nation; and as I have heard, some have got their children Baptized by the Popish Priest, for there has been no Chaplain here for above these four years.'—Public Archives, Canada. Nova Scotia A, vol. xxv, p. 176.

the French troops desired to winter at Chignecto, the Acadians objected and persuaded them to leave, which 'made their conduct appear to have been on this occasion far better than could have been expected from them.'[25] Once more the Acadians resumed their work on the fortifications and supplied the garrison with provisions. They frankly admitted giving assistance to the French, but produced an order from the Sieur du Vivier threatening them with punishment at the hands of the Indians if they refused.

In May of the following year (1745) a party of Canadians and Indians, under the raider Marin, invested Annapolis. Again the Acadians refused to take up arms and again assisted the invaders with supplies. By the end of the month, however, Marin and his raiders had vanished and the garrison at Annapolis saw them no more. They had been urgently summoned by the governor of Ile Royale to come to his assistance, for Louisbourg was even then in dire peril. An army of New Englanders under Pepperrell, supported by a squadron of the British Navy under Warren, had in fact laid siege to the fortress in the same month.[26] But Marin's raiders could render no effective service. On the forty-ninth day of the siege Louisbourg surrendered to the English,[27] and shortly afterwards the entire French population, civil and military, among them many Acadians, were transported to France.

The fall of Louisbourg and the removal of the inhabitants alarmed the French authorities, who now entertained fears for the safety of Canada and determined to take steps for the recapture of the lost stronghold, and with it the whole of Acadia, in the following year. Accordingly, a formidable fleet, under the command of the Duc d'Anville, sailed from La Rochelle in June 1746; while the governor of Quebec sent a strong detachment of fighting Canadians under Ramesay to

---

[25] Nova Scotia Documents, p. 147.

[26] See The Great Fortress in this Series, chap. ii.

[27] June 17, Old Style, June 28, New Style, 1745. The English at this time still used the Old Style Julian calendar, while the French used the Gregorian, New Style. Hence some of the disagreement in respect to dates which we find in the various accounts of this period.

assist in the intended siege. But disaster after disaster overtook the fleet. A violent tempest scattered the ships in mid-ocean and an epidemic carried off hundreds of seamen and soldiers. In the autumn the commander, with a remnant of his ships, arrived in Chebucto Bay (Halifax), where he himself died. The battered ships finally put back to France, and nothing came of the enterprise.[28] Meanwhile, rumours having reached Quebec of a projected invasion of Canada by New England troops, the governor Beauharnois had recalled Ramesay's Canadians for the defence of Quebec; but on hearing that the French ships had arrived in Chebucto Bay, and expecting them to attack Annapolis, Ramesay marched his forces into the heart of Acadia in order to be on hand to support the fleet. Then, when the failure of the fleet became apparent, he retired to Beaubassin at the head of Chignecto Bay, and proceeded to fortify the neck of the peninsula, building a fort at Baie Verte on the eastern shore. He was joined by a considerable band of Malecites and Micmacs under the Abbe Le Loutre; and emissaries were sent out among the Acadians as far as Minas to persuade them to take up arms on the side of the French.

William Shirley, the governor of Massachusetts, who exercised supervision over the affairs of Nova Scotia, seeing in this a real menace to British power in the colony, raised a thousand New Englanders and dispatched them to Annapolis. Of these only four hundred and seventy, under Colonel Arthur Noble of Massachusetts, arrived at their destination. Most of the vessels carrying the others were wrecked by storms; one was driven back by a French warship. In December, however, Noble's New Englanders, with a few soldiers from the Annapolis garrison, set out to rid Acadia of the Canadians; and after much hardship and toil finally reached the village of Grand Pre in the district of Minas. Here the soldiers were quartered in the houses of the Acadians for the winter, for Noble had decided to postpone the movement against Ramesay's position on the isthmus until spring. It would be impossible, he thought, to make the march through the snow.

---

[28] See The Great Fortress, chap. iii.

But the warlike Canadians whom Ramesay had posted in the neck of land between Chignecto Bay and Baie Verte did not think so. No sooner had they learned of Noble's position at Grand Pre than they resolved to surprise him by a forced march and an attack by night. Friendly Acadians warned the British of the intended surprise; but the over-confident Noble scouted the idea. The snow in many places was 'twelve to sixteen feet deep,' and no party, even of Canadians, thought Noble, could possibly make a hundred miles of forest in such a winter. So it came to pass that one midnight, early in February, Noble's men in Grand Pre found themselves surrounded. After a plucky fight in which sixty English were killed, among them Colonel Noble, and seventy more wounded, Captain Benjamin Goldthwaite, who had assumed the command, surrendered. The enemies then, to all appearances, became the best of friends. The victorious Canadians sat down to eat and drink with the defeated New Englanders, who made, says Beaujeu, one of the Canadian officers, 'many compliments on our polite manners and our skill in making war.' The English prisoners were allowed to return to Annapolis with the honours of war, while their sick and wounded were cared for by the victors. This generosity Mascarene afterwards gratefully acknowledged.

When the Canadians returned to Chignecto with the report of their victory over the British, Ramesay issued a proclamation to the inhabitants of Grand Pre setting forth that 'by virtue of conquest they now owed allegiance to the King of France,' and warning them 'to hold no communication with the inhabitants of Port Royal.' This proclamation, however, had little effect. With few exceptions the Acadians maintained their former attitude and refused to bear arms, even on behalf of France and in the presence of French troops. 'There were,' says Mascarene, 'in the last action some of those inhabitants, but none of any account belonging to this province... The generality of the inhabitants of this province possess still the same fidelity they have done before, in which I endeavour to encourage them.'

Quite naturally, however, there was some unrest among the Acadians. After the capture of Louisbourg in 1745 the British had transported all the inhabitants of that place to France; and rumours were afloat of an expedition for the conquest of

Canada and that the Acadians were to share a similar fate. This being made known to the British ministry, the Duke of Newcastle wrote to Governor Shirley of Massachusetts, instructing him to issue a proclamation assuring the Acadians 'that there is not the least foundation for any apprehension of that nature: but that on the contrary it is His Majesty's resolution to protect and maintain all such of them as shall continue in their duty and allegiance to His Majesty in the quiet and peaceable possession of their habitations and settlements and that they shall continue to enjoy the free exercise of their religion.'[29]

Shirley proceeded to give effect to this order. He issued a proclamation informing the inhabitants of the intention of the king towards them; omitting, however, that clause relating to their religion, a clause all-important to them. The document was printed at Boston in French, and sent to Mascarene to be distributed. Mascarene thought at the time that it produced a good effect. Shirley's instructions were clear; but in explanation of his omission he represented that such a promise might cause inconvenience, as it was desirable to wean the Acadians from their attachment to the French and the influence of the bishop of Quebec. He contended, moreover, that the Treaty of Utrecht did not guarantee the free exercise of religion. In view of this explanation,[30] Shirley's action was approved by the king.

In Shirley's proclamation several persons were indicted for high treason,[31] and a reward of 50 pounds was offered for the capture of any one offender named. These, apparently, were the only pronounced rebels in the province. There were more sputterings in Acadia of the relentless war that raged between New France and New England. Shirley had sent another detachment of troops in April to reoccupy Grand Pre; and the governor of Quebec had sent another war-party. But in the next year (1748) the Treaty of Aix-la-Chapelle, by which Ile

---

[29] Newcastle to Shirley, May 30, 1747.—Canadian Archives Report, 1905, Appendix C, vol. ii, p. 47.
[30] Bedford to Shirley, May 10, 1748.
[31] Canadian Archives Report, 1906, Appendix C, vol. ii, p. 48.

Royale (Cape Breton) and Ile St Jean (Prince Edward Island) were restored to France, brought hostilities to a pause.

CHAPTER V

CORNWALLIS AND THE ACADIANS

In Nova Scotia England was weak from the fact that no settlements of her own people had been established there. After thirty years of British rule Mascarene had written, 'There is no number of English inhabitants settled in this province worth mentioning, except the five companies here [at Annapolis] and four at Canso.' Now the restoration to France of Cape Breton with the fortress of Louisbourg exposed Nova Scotia to attack; and in time of war with France the Acadians would be a source of weakness rather than of strength. Great Britain, therefore, resolved to try the experiment of forming in Nova Scotia a colony of her own sons.

Thus it came to pass that a fleet of transports carrying over twenty-five hundred colonists, counting women and children, escorted by a sloop-of-war, cast anchor in Chebucto Bay in July 1749. This expedition was commanded by Edward Cornwallis, the newly appointed governor and captain-general of Nova Scotia. He was a young officer of thirty-six, twin-brother of the Rev. Frederick Cornwallis, afterwards Archbishop of Canterbury, and uncle of the more famous Lord Cornwallis who surrendered at Yorktown thirty-two years later. With the colonists came many officers and disbanded soldiers; came, also, the soldiers of the garrison which had occupied Louisbourg before the peace; for the new settlement, named Halifax in honour of the president of the Lords of Trade, was to be a military stronghold, as well as a naval base, and the seat of government for the province.

While Cornwallis and his colonists laid the foundations of Halifax, cleared the land, formed the streets, put up their dwellings and defences, and organized their government, the home authorities took up the problem of securing more settlers for Nova Scotia. Cornwallis had been instructed to prepare for settlements at Minas, La Heve, Whitehead, and Baie Verte, the intention being that the newcomers should eventually absorb the Acadians living at these places. It had been suggested to the Lords of Trade, probably by John Dick, a merchant of

Rotterdam, that the most effective means to this end would be to introduce a large French Protestant element into Nova Scotia. The government thereupon gave instructions that the land should be surveyed and plans prepared dividing the territory into alternate Protestant and Catholic sections. Through intercourse and intermarriage with neighbours speaking their own tongue, it was fondly hoped that the Acadians, in course of time, would become loyal British subjects. The next step was to secure French Protestant emigrants. In December 1749 the Lords of Trade entered into a contract with John Dick to transport 'not more than fifteen hundred foreign Protestants to Nova Scotia.'[32] Dick was a man of energy and resource and, in business methods, somewhat in advance of his age. He appears to have understood the value of advertising, judging from the handbills which he circulated in France and from his advertisements in the newspapers. But as time passed emigrants in anything like the numbers expected were not forthcoming. Evil reports concerning Nova Scotia had been circulated in France, and other difficulties arose. After many delays, however, two hundred and eighty persons recruited by Dick arrived at Halifax. The character of some gave rise to complaint, and Dick was cautioned by the government. His troubles in France crept on apace. It began to be rumoured that the emigrants were being enrolled in the Halifax militia; and, France being no longer a profitable field, Dick transferred his activities to Germany. Alluring handbills in the German tongue were circulated, and in the end a considerable number of Teutons arrived at Halifax. Most of these were afterwards settled at Lunenburg. The enterprise, of course, failed of its object to neutralize and eventually assimilate the Acadian Catholic population; nevertheless several thousand excellent 'foreign Protestant' settlers reached Nova Scotia through various channels. They were given land in different parts of the province and in time became good citizens.

Cornwallis's instructions from the British ministry contained many clauses relating to the Acadians. Though they

[32] Public Archives, Canada. Nova Scotia A, vol. xxxv, p. 189.

had given assistance to the enemy, they should be permitted to remain in the possession of their property. They must, however, take the oath of allegiance 'within three months from the date of the declaration' which the governor was to make. Liberty of conscience should be permitted to all. In the event of any of the inhabitants wishing to leave the province, the governor should remind them that the time allowed under the Treaty of Utrecht for the removal of their property had long since expired. The governor should take particular care that 'they do no damage, before such their removal, to their respective homes and plantations.' Determined efforts should be made, not only to Anglicize, but to Protestantize the people. Marriages between the Acadians and the English were to be encouraged. Trade with the French settlements was prohibited. No episcopal jurisdiction might be exercised in the province, a mandate intended to shut out the bishop of Quebec. Every facility was to be given for the education of Acadian children in Protestant schools. Those who embraced Protestantism were to be confirmed in their lands, free from quit-rent for a period of ten years.[33]

Armed with these instructions, Cornwallis adopted at first a strong policy. On July 14, 1749, he issued a proclamation containing 'the declaration of His Majesty regarding the French inhabitants of Nova Scotia,' and calling on the Acadians to take the oath of allegiance within three months. At a meeting of the Council held the same day, at which representatives of the Acadians were present, the document was discussed. The deputies listened with some concern to the declaration, and inquired whether permission would be given them to sell their lands if they decided to leave the country. The governor replied that under the Treaty of Utrecht they had enjoyed this privilege for one year only, and that they could not now 'be allowed to sell or carry off anything.' The deputies asked for time to consult the inhabitants. This was granted, with a warning that those who 'should not take the oath of allegiance before the 15th of October should forfeit all their possessions and rights in the Province.' Deputies from nine districts appeared before

---

[33] Canadian Archives Report, 1905, Appendix C, vol. ii, p. 50.

the Council on July 31 and spoke for the Acadians. The Council deliberated and decided that no priest should officiate without a licence from the governor; that no exemption from bearing arms in time of war could be made; that the oath must be taken as offered; and that all who wished to continue in the possession of their lands must appear and take the oath before October 15, which would be the last day allowed them.[34]

A month later they presented to Cornwallis a petition signed by one thousand inhabitants to the effect that they had faithfully served King George, and were prepared to renew the oath which was tendered to them by Governor Philipps; that two years before His Majesty had promised to maintain them in the peaceable enjoyment of their possessions: 'And we believe, Your Excellency, that if His Majesty had been informed of our conduct towards His Majesty's Government, he would not propose to us an oath which, if taken, would at any moment expose our lives to great peril from the savage nations, who have reproached us in a strange manner as to the oath we have taken to His Majesty... But if Your Excellency is not disposed to grant us what we take the liberty of asking, we are resolved, every one of us, to leave the country.' In reply Cornwallis reminded them that, as British subjects, they were in the enjoyment of their religion and in possession of their property. 'You tell me that General Philipps granted you the reservation which you demand; and I tell you gentlemen, that the general who granted you such reservation did not do his duty... You have been for more than thirty-four years past the subjects of the King of Great Britain... Show now that you are grateful.'[35]

The Acadians, however, showed still a decided aversion to an unqualified oath; and Cornwallis apparently thought it best to recede somewhat from the high stand he had taken. He wrote to the home government explaining that he hesitated to carry out the terms of his proclamation of July 14 by confiscating the property of those who did not take the oath, on the ground that the Acadians would not emigrate at that season of the year, and that in the meantime he could employ

[34] Public Archives, Canada. Nova Scotia B, vol. iv, p. 14.
[35] Public Archives, Canada. Nova Scotia B, vol. iv, p. 49.

them to advantage. If they continued to prove obstinate, he would seek new instructions to force things to a conclusion.[36] The Acadians, used by this time to the lenity of the British government, were probably not surprised to find, at the meeting of the Council held on October 11, no mention of the oath which had to be taken before the 15th of the month.

The winter passed, and still Cornwallis took no steps to enforce his proclamation. He had his troubles; for the French, from Quebec on the one side and from Louisbourg on the other, were fomenting strife; and the Indians were on the war-path. And, in February 1750, the Lords of Trade wrote that as the French were forming new settlements with a view to enticing the Acadians into them, any forcible means of ejecting them should be waived for the present. Cornwallis replied that he was anxious to leave matters in abeyance until he ascertained what could be done in the way of fortifying Chignecto. 'If a fort is once built there,' he explained, 'they [the Indians] will be driven out of the peninsula or submit. He also wished to know what reinforcements he might expect in the spring. Until then he would 'defer making the inhabitants take the oath of allegiance.'

Meanwhile the Acadians were not idle on their own behalf. In October 1749 they addressed a memorial to Des Herbiers, the governor of Ile Royale, to be transmitted to the French king. They complained that the new governor intended to suppress their missionaries,[37] and to force them to bear arms against the Indians, with whom they had always been on friendly terms. They therefore prayed the king to obtain concessions from Great Britain—the maintenance of the Quebec missionaries, the exemption from bearing arms, or an extension of a year in which they might withdraw with their effects.[38] Two months later they sent a petition to the Marquis

---

[36] Public Archives, Canada. Nova Scotia A, vol. xxxv, p. 48.
[37] Cornwallis had denied the jurisdiction of the bishop of Quebec, but had intimated that he would grant a licence to any good priest, his objection being to missionaries such as Le Loutre, who stirred up the Indians to commit hostilities.
[38] Canadian Archives Report, 1905, Appendix N, vol. ii, p. 298.

de la Jonquiere, the governor of Canada, actuated, they said, by the love of their country and their religion. They had refused to take the oath requiring them to bear arms against their fellow-countrymen. They had, it is true, appeared attached to the interests of the English, in consequence of the oath which they had consented to take only when exempted from bearing arms. Now that this exemption was removed, they wished to leave Nova Scotia, and hoped that the king would help them with vessels, as they had been refused permission to build them. Great offers had been made to them, but they preferred to leave.[39]

In the spring of 1750, unable to obtain permission from Cornwallis to take a restricted oath, the Acadians almost unanimously decided to emigrate. On April 19 deputies from several settlements in the district of Minas—the river Canard, Grand Pre, and Pisiquid—appeared before the Council at Halifax and asked to be allowed to leave the province with their effects.[40] According to Cornwallis, they professed that this decision was taken against their inclination, and that the French had threatened them with destruction at the hands of the Indians if they remained.[41] On May 25 the inhabitants of Annapolis Royal came with a like petition.

In reply to these petitions Cornwallis reminded the inhabitants that the province was the country of their fathers, and that they should enjoy the product of their labours. As soon as there should be tranquillity he would give them permission to depart, if they wished to do so; but in the present circumstances passports could not be granted to any one. They could not be permitted to strengthen the hand of Great Britain's enemy.

But in spite of the prohibition, of the forts that were built to enforce it, and of British cruisers patrolling the coasts to prevent intercourse with the French, there was a considerable emigration. A number of families crossed to Ile St Jean in the summer of 1750. They were aided by the missionaries, and

[39] Ibid., p. 301.
[40] Public Archives, Canada. Nova Scotia B, vol. iv, p. 130.
[41] Public Archives, Canada. Nova Scotia A, vol. xxxvii, p. 7.

supplied with vessels and arms by the French authorities at Louisbourg. By August 1750 we know that eight hundred Acadians were settled in Ile St Jean.

CHAPTER VI

THE 'ANCIENT BOUNDARIES'

By the terms of the Treaty of Aix-la-Chapelle the question of the limits of Acadia had been referred to a commission of arbitration, and each of the powers had agreed to attempt no settlement on the debatable ground until such time as the decision of the commissioners should be made known. Each, however, continued to watch jealously over its own interests. The English persisted in their claim that the ancient boundaries included all the country north of the Bay of Fundy to the St Lawrence, and Cornwallis was directed to see to it that no subjects of the French king settled within these boundaries. The French, on the other hand, steadily asserted their ownership in all land north of a line drawn from Baie Verte to Chignecto Bay. The disputants, though openly at peace, glowered at each other. Hardly had Cornwallis brought his colonists ashore at Halifax, when La Galissoniere, the acting-governor of Canada, sent Boishebert, with a detachment of twenty men, to the river St John, to assert the French claim to that district; and when La Galissoniere went to France as a commissioner in the boundary dispute, his successor, La Jonquiere, dispatched a force under the Chevalier de la Corne to occupy the isthmus of Chignecto.

About the same time the Indians went on the war-path, apparently at the instigation of the French. Des Herbiers, the governor of Ile Royale, when dispatching the Abbe Le Loutre to the savages with the usual presents, had added blankets and a supply of powder and ball, clearly intended to aid them should they be disposed to attack the English settlements. Indians from the river St John joined the Micmacs and opened hostilities by seizing an English vessel at Canso and taking twenty prisoners. The prisoners were liberated by Des Herbiers; but the Micmacs, their blood up, assembled at Chignecto, near La Corne's post, and declared war on the English. The Council at Halifax promptly raised several companies for defence, and offered a reward of 10 pounds for the capture of an Indian, dead or alive. Cornwallis complained bitterly to Louisbourg that

Le Loutre was stirring up trouble; but Des Herbiers disingenuously disclaimed all responsibility for the abbe. The Indians, he said, were merely allies, not French subjects, and Le Loutre acted under the direction of the governor of Canada. He promised also that if any Frenchman molested the English, he should be punished, a promise which, as subsequent events showed, he had no intention of keeping.

In November 1749 a party of one hundred and fifty Indians captured a company of engineers at Grand Pre, where the English had just built a fort. Le Loutre, however, ransomed the prisoners and sent them to Louisbourg. The Indians, emboldened by their success, then issued a proclamation in the name of the king of France and their Indian allies calling upon the Acadians to arm, under pain of death for disobedience. On learning that eleven Acadians obeyed this summons, Cornwallis sent Captain Goreham of the Rangers to arrest them. The rebels, however, made good their escape, thanks to the Indians; and Goreham could only make prisoners of some of their children, whom he brought before the governor. The children declared that their parents had not been free agents, and produced in evidence one of the threatening orders of the Indians. In any case, of course, the children were in no way responsible, and were therefore sent home; and the governor described Goreham as 'no officer at all.'

When spring came Cornwallis took steps to stop the incursions of the savages and at the same time to check the emigration of the Acadians. He sent detachments to build and occupy fortified posts at Grand Pre, at Pisiquid, and at other places. He ordered Major Lawrence to sail up the Bay of Fundy with four hundred settlers for Beaubassin, the Acadian village at the head of Chignecto Bay. For the time being, however, this undertaking did not prosper. On arriving, Lawrence encountered a band of Micmacs, which Le Loutre had posted at the dikes to resist the disembarkation. Some fighting ensued before Lawrence succeeded in leading ashore a body of troops. The motive of the turbulent abbe was to preserve the Acadians from the contaminating presence of heretics and enemies of his master, the French king. And, when he saw that he could not prevent the English from making a lodgment in the village, he went forward with his Micmacs and set it on fire, thus forcing the Acadian inhabitants to cross to the French camp at Beausejour, some two miles off. Here La Corne had set up his standard to mark the boundary of New France, beyond which he dared the British to advance at their peril. At a conference which was arranged between Lawrence and La Corne, La Corne said that the governor of Canada, La Jonquiere, had directed him to take possession of the country to the north, 'or at least he was to keep it and must defend it till the boundaries between the two Crowns should be settled.'[42] Moreover, if Lawrence should try to effect a settlement, La Corne would oppose it to the last. And as Lawrence's forces were quite inadequate to cope with La Corne's, it only remained for Lawrence to return to Halifax with his troops and settlers.

Meanwhile Boishebert stood guard for the governor of Quebec at the mouth of the river St John. In the previous year, when he had arrived there, Cornwallis had sent an officer to protest against what he considered an encroachment; but Boishebert had answered simply that he was commissioned to hold the place for his royal master without attempting a settlement until the boundary dispute should be adjusted. Now, in July 1750, Captain Cobb of the York, cruising in the Bay of Fundy, sighted a French sloop near the mouth of the St John, and opened fire. The French captain immediately lowered his boats and landed a party of sailors, apparently with the intention of coming to a conference. Cobb followed his example. Presently Boishebert came forward under a flag of truce and demanded Cobb's authority for the act of war in territory claimed by the French. Cobb produced his commission and handed it to Boishebert. Keeping the document in his possession, Boishebert ordered Cobb to bring his vessel under the stern of the French sloop, and sent French officers to board Cobb's ship and see the order carried out. The sailors on the York, however, held the Frenchmen as hostages for the safe return of their captain. After some parleying Cobb was allowed to return to his vessel, and the Frenchmen were released. Boishebert, however, refused to return the captain's

[42] Canadian Archives Report, 1906, Appendix N, vol. ii, p. 321.

commission. Cobb thereupon boarded the French sloop, seized five of the crew, and sailed away.

So the game went on. A month later the British sloop Trial, at Baie Verte, captured a French sloop of seventy tons which was engaged in carrying arms and supplies to Le Loutre's Indians. On board were four deserters from the British and a number of Acadians. Among the papers found on the Acadians were letters addressed to their friends in Quebec and others from Le Loutre and officers of Fort St John and of Port La Joie in Ile St Jean. From one of these letters we obtain a glimpse of the conditions of the Acadians:

> I shall tell you that I was settled in Acadia. I have four small children. I lived contented on my land. But that did not last long, for we were compelled to leave all our property and flee from under the domination of the English. The King undertakes to transport us and support us under the expectation of news from France. If Acadia is not restored to France I hope to take my little family and bring it to Canada. I beg you to let me know the state of things in that country. I assure you that we are in poor condition, for we are like the Indians in the woods.[43]

By other documents taken it was shown that supplies from Quebec were frequently passing to the Indians, and that the dispatches addressed to Cornwallis were intercepted and forwarded to the governor of Quebec.[44]

These papers revealed to Cornwallis the peril which menaced him. But, having been reinforced by the arrival from Newfoundland of three hundred men of Lascelles's regiment, he resolved to occupy Chignecto, which Lawrence had been forced to abandon in April. Accordingly Lawrence again set out, this time with about seven hundred men. In mid-September his ships appeared off the burnt village of Beaubassin. Again the landing was opposed by a band of

---

[43] A. Doucet to Mde Langedo of Quebec, August 5, 1750.
[44] Cornwallis to Bedford, August 19, 1750.

Indians and about thirty Acadians entrenched on the shore. These, after some fighting and losses, were beaten off; and the English troops landed and proceeded to construct a fort, named by them Fort Lawrence, and to erect barracks for the winter. La Corne, from his fort at Beausejour, where he had his troops and a body of Acadians, addressed a note to Lawrence, proposing a meeting in a boat in the middle of the river. Lawrence replied that he had no business with La Corne, and that La Corne could come to him if he had anything to communicate. Acts of violence followed. It was not long before a scouting party under the command of Captain Bartelot was surrounded by a band of Indians and Acadians.[45] Forty-five of the party were killed, and Bartelot and eight men were taken prisoners. A few weeks later there was an act of treachery which greatly embittered the British soldiers. This was the murder of Captain Howe, one of the British officers, by some of Le Loutre's Micmacs. It was stated that Le Loutre was personally implicated in the crime, but there appears not the slightest foundation for this charge. One morning in October Howe saw an Indian carrying a flag of truce on the opposite side of the Missaguash river, which lay between Fort Lawrence and Fort Beausejour. Howe, who had often held converse with the savages, went forward to meet the Indian, and the two soon became engaged in conversation. Suddenly the Indian lowered his flag, a body of savages concealed behind a dike opened fire, and Howe fell, mortally wounded. In the work of bringing the dying officer into the fort ten of his company also fell.

Meanwhile an event occurred which seemed likely to promote more cordial relations between the French and the English. Early in October Des Herbiers returned to Halifax thirty- seven prisoners, including six women, who had been captured by the Indians but ransomed and sent to Louisbourg by the Abbe Le Loutre. It is difficult to reconcile the conduct of the meddlesome missionary on this occasion with what we know of his character. He was possessed of an inveterate

---

[45] La Valliere, one of the French officers on the spot, says that the Indians and Acadians were encouraged by Le Loutre during this attack.—Journal of the Sieur de la Valliere.

hatred of the English and all their works; yet he was capable of an act of humanity towards them. After all, it may be that generosity was not foreign to the nature of this fanatical French patriot. Cornwallis was grateful, and cheerfully refunded the amount of the ransom.[46]

But the harmony existing between Des Herbiers and Cornwallis was of short duration. In the same month the British sloop Albany, commanded by Captain Rous, fell on the French brigantine St Francois, Captain Vergor, on the southern coast. Vergor, who was carrying stores and ammunition to Louisbourg, ran up his colours, but after a fight of three hours he was forced by Rous to surrender. The captive ship was taken to Halifax and there condemned as a prize, the cargo being considered contraband of war. La Jonquiere addressed a peremptory letter to Cornwallis, demanding whether he was acting under orders in seizing a French vessel in French territory. He likewise instructed Des Herbiers to seize ships of the enemy; and as a result four prizes were sold by the Admiralty Court at Louisbourg.

Open hostilities soon became the order of the day. During the winter a party of Canadians and Indians and Acadians disguised as Indians assembled near Fort Lawrence. They succeeded in killing two men, and continued to fire on the British position for two days. But, as the garrison remained within the shelter of the walls, the attackers grew weary of wasting ammunition and withdrew to harry the settlement at Halifax. According to the French accounts, these savages killed thirty persons on the outskirts of Halifax in the spring of 1751, and Cornwallis reported that four inhabitants and six soldiers had been taken prisoners. Then in June three hundred British troops from Fort Lawrence invaded the French territory to attempt a surprise. They were discovered, however, and St Ours, who had succeeded La Corne, brought out his forces and drove them back to Fort Lawrence. A month later the British made another attack and destroyed a dike, flooding the lands of the Acadians in its neighbourhood.

---

[46] Des Herbiers to Cornwallis, October 2, 1750.—Public Archives, Canada. Nova Scotia A, vol. xxxix, p. 13.

And during all this time England and France were theoretically at peace. Their commissioners sat in Paris, La Galissoniere on one side, Shirley on the other, piling up mountains of argument as to the 'ancient boundaries' of Acadia. All to no purpose; for neither nation could afford to recede from its position. It was a question for the last argument of kings. Meanwhile the officials in the colonies anxiously waited for the decision; and the poor Acadians, torn between the hostile camps, and many of them now homeless, waited too.

CHAPTER VII

A LULL IN THE CONFLICT

The years 1752 and 1753 were, on the whole, years of peace and quiet. This was largely due to changes in the administration on both sides. At the end of 1751 the Count de Raymond had replaced Des Herbiers as governor of Ile Royale; in 1752 Duquesne succeeded La Jonquiere at Quebec as governor of New France; and Peregrine Hopson took the place of Cornwallis in the government of Nova Scotia. Hopson adopted a policy of conciliation. When the crew of a New England schooner in the summer of 1752 killed an Indian lad and two girls whom they had enticed on board, Hopson promptly offered a reward for the capture of the culprits. He treated the Indians with such consistent kindness that he was able in the month of September to form an alliance with the Micmacs on the coast. He established friendly relations also with Duquesne and Raymond, and arranged with them a cartel of exchange regarding deserters.

Towards the Acadians Hopson seemed most sympathetic. From the experience of Cornwallis he knew, of course, their aversion to the oath of allegiance. In writing to the Lords of Trade for instructions he pointed out the obstinacy of the people on this question, but made it clear how necessary their presence was to the welfare of the province. Meanwhile he did his best to conciliate them. When complaints were made that Captain Hamilton, a British officer, had carried off some of their cattle, Hamilton was reprimanded and the cattle were paid for. Instructions were then issued to all officers to treat the Acadians as British subjects, and to take nothing from them by force. Should the people refuse to comply with any just demand, the officer must report it to the governor and await his orders. When the Acadians provided wood for the garrison, certificates must be issued which should entitle them to payment.

The political horizon at the opening of the year 1753 seemed bright to Hopson. But in the spring a most painful occurrence threatened for a time to involve him in an Indian war. Two men, Connor and Grace, while cruising off the coast, had landed at Ile Dore, and with the assistance of their ruffianly crew had plundered an Indian storehouse. They were overtaken by a storm, their schooner became a total wreck, and Connor and Grace alone survived. They were rescued by the Indians, who cared for them and gave them shelter. But the miserable cowards seized a favourable moment to murder and scalp their benefactors. Well satisfied with their brutal act, they proceeded to Halifax with the ghastly trophies, and boldly demanded payment for the scalps of two men, three women, and two children. Their story seemed so improbable that the Council ordered them to give security to appear in the court at the next general session.[47] The prospect of a permanent peace with the Indians vanished. They demanded that the Council should send a schooner to Ile Dore to protect their shores. The Council did send a vessel. But no sooner had it arrived than the Indians seized and massacred the whole crew save one man, who claimed to be of French origin and was later ransomed by the French.

In September the inhabitants of Grand Pre, Canso, and Pisiquid presented a petition to the Council at Halifax, praying that their missionaries be excused from taking the ordinary oath. The Acadians were entitled to the free exercise of their religion, and the bishop of Quebec would not send priests if they were required to become British subjects. The Council deliberated. Fearing to give the Acadians a pretext for leaving the country on the plea that they had been deprived of the services of their priests, the Council decided to grant the petition, providing, however, that the priests should obtain a licence from the governor.

The Lords of Trade approved Hopson's policy, which appeared to be bearing good fruit. Later in the autumn came another delegation of Acadians who had formerly resided at Pisiquid but had migrated to French territory, asking to be allowed to return to their old homes. They had left on account

---

[47] Hopson to Lords of Trade, April 30, 1753, p. 30. Deposition of Connor and Grace, April 16, 1753, p. 30 et seq.—Public Archives, Canada. Nova Scotia A, vol. liii.

of the severe oath proposed by Cornwallis, but were now willing to come back and take a restricted oath. For fear of the Indians, they could not swear to bear arms in aid of the English in time of war. They wished also to be able to move from the province whenever they desired, and to take their effects with them. Evidently they had not found Utopia under the French flag. The Council gave them the permission they desired, promised them the free exercise of their religion, a sufficient number of priests for their needs, and all the privileges conferred by the Treaty of Utrecht.

On the whole, the situation in the autumn of 1753 was most promising. The Acadians, said Hopson, behaved 'tolerably well,' though they still feared the Indians should they attach themselves to the English. Of the French on the frontier there was nothing to complain; and an era of peace seemed assured. But before the end of the year another page in the history of Nova Scotia had been turned. Raymond, the governor of Ile Royale, gave place to D'Ailleboust. Hopson was compelled to return to England on leave of absence through failing eyesight, and Charles Lawrence reigned in his stead.

CHAPTER VIII

THE LAWRENCE REGIME

The policy both of France and of England towards the Acadians was based upon political expediency rather than upon any definite or well-conceived plan for the development of the country. The inhabitants, born to serve rather than to command, had honestly striven according to their light to maintain respect for constituted authority. But the state of unrest into which they were so frequently thrown had deprived them of all sense of security in their homes and had created among them a spirit of suspicion. Unable to reason, disinclined to rebel, they had settled down into a morose intractability, while their confidence in the generosity or even in the justice of their rulers gradually disappeared. Those who could have restored them to a normal condition of healthy citizenship saw fit to keep them in disquietude, holding over their heads the tomahawk of the Indian. England and France were nominally at peace. But each nation was only waiting for a favourable moment to strike a decisive blow, not merely for Acadia or any part of it, but for the mastery of the North American continent. With this object ever in the background, France, through her agents, strove to make the Acadians a thorn in Great Britain's side, while England hesitated to allow them to pass over to the ranks of her enemies. At the same time she was anxious that they should, by some visible sign, acknowledge her sovereignty. But to become a British subject it was necessary to take the oath of allegiance. Most of the Acadians had refused to take this oath without reservations. Great Britain should then have allowed them to depart or should have deported them. She had done neither. On the contrary, she had tried to keep them, had made concessions to them to remain, and had closed her eyes to violations of the law, until many of them had been, by various means, acknowledged as British subjects.

A Murray or a Dorchester would have humoured the people and would probably have kept them in allegiance. But this was an impossible task for Lawrence. He was unaccustomed to compromise. He kept before him the letter of the law, and believed that any deviation from it was fraught with danger. He entered upon his duties as administrator in the month of October 1753. Six weeks later he made a report on the condition of affairs in the province. This report contains one pregnant sentence. He is referring to the emigrant Acadians who had left their homes for French soil and were now wishing to come back, and he says: 'But Your Lordships may be assured they will never have my consent to return until they comply [take the oath] without any reservation whatever.'[48] This was the keynote of all Lawrence's subsequent action. The Acadians must take the oath without reserve, or leave the country. He does not appear to have given any consideration to the fact that for forty years the Lords of Trade had, for various motives, nursed the people, or that only two years before the Council at Halifax had declared the Acadians to be still entitled to the privileges accorded to them by the Treaty of Utrecht. To him the Acadians were as an enemy in the camp, and as such they were to be treated.

The Lords of Trade partly acquiesced in Lawrence's reasoning, yet they warned him to be cautious. A year before they had announced that those who remained in the country were to be considered as holding good titles; but they now maintained that the inhabitants had 'in fact no right, but upon condition of taking the oath of allegiance absolute and unqualified.' Officials might be sent among them to inquire into their disputes, but 'the more we consider the point, the more nice and difficult it appears to us; for, as on the one hand great caution ought to be used to avoid giving alarm and creating such a diffidence in their minds as might induce them to quit the province, and by their numbers add strength to the French settlements, so on the other hand we should be equally cautious of creating an improper and false confidence in them, that by a perseverance in refusing to take the oath of allegiance, they may gradually work out in their own way a right to their lands and to the benefit and protection of the law, which they are not entitled to but on that condition.'[49]

---

[48] Lawrence to Lords of Trade, December 5, 1753.
[49] Lords of Trade to Lawrence, March 4, 1754.

After nine months' tenure of office Lawrence had fully made up his mind as to his policy in dealing with the Acadians. On August 1, 1754, he addressed a letter to the Lords of Trade, to acquaint them with the measures which appeared to him to be 'the most practicable and effectual for putting a stop to the many inconveniences we have long laboured under, from their obstinacy, treachery, partiality to their own countrymen, and their ingratitude for the favour, indulgence, and protection they have at all times so undeservedly received from His Majesty's Government. Your Lordships well know that they always affected a neutrality, and as it has been generally imagined here that the mildness of an English Government would by degrees have fixed them in their own interest, no violent measures have ever been taken with them. But I must observe to Your Lordships that this lenity has not had the least good effect; on the contrary, I believe they have at present laid aside all thoughts of taking the oaths voluntarily, and great numbers of them at present are gone to Beausejour to work for the French, in order to dyke out the water at the settlement.'[50]

Lawrence explained that he had offered the Acadians work at Halifax, which they had refused to accept; and that he had then issued a proclamation calling upon them 'to return forthwith to their lands as they should answer the contrary at their peril.' Moreover, 'They have not for a long time brought anything to our markets, but on the other hand have carried everything to the French and Indians whom they have always assisted with provisions, quarters, and intelligence. And indeed while they remain without taking the oaths to His Majesty (which they never will do till they are forced) and have incendiary French priests among them there are no hopes of their amendment. As they possess the best and largest tracts of land in this province, it cannot be settled with any effect while they remain in this situation. And tho' I would be very far from attempting such a step without Your Lordships' approbation, yet I cannot help being of opinion that it would be much better, if they refuse the oaths, that they were away. The only ill consequences that can attend their going would be their taking

---

[50] Lawrence to Lords of Trade, August 1, 1754.

arms and joining with the Indians to distress our settlements, as they are numerous and our troops are much divided; tho' indeed I believe that a very large part of the inhabitants would submit to any terms rather than take up arms on either side; but that is only my conjecture, and not to be depended upon in so critical a circumstance. However, if Your Lordships should be of opinion that we are not sufficiently established to take so important a step, we could prevent any inconvenience by building a fort or a few blockhouses on Chibenacadie [Shubenacadie] river. It would hinder in a great measure their communication with the French.'

In order to prevent the Acadians from trading with the French, Lawrence issued a proclamation forbidding the exportation of corn from the province, imposing a penalty of fifty pounds for each offence, half of such sum to be paid to the informer. The exact purpose of the proclamation was explained in a circular. First, it was to prevent 'the supplying of corn to the Indians and their abettors, who, residing on the north side of the Bay of Fundy, do commit hostilities upon His Majesty's subjects which they cannot so conveniently do, that supply being cut off.' Secondly, it was for the better supply of the Halifax market, which had been obliged to supply itself from other colonies. The inhabitants were not asked to sell their corn to any particular person or at any fixed price; all that was insisted upon was their supplying the Halifax market before they should think of sending corn elsewhere. There was, of course, nothing objectionable in this proclamation. It was only a protective measure for the benefit of the whole colony, and did 'not bind the French inhabitants more or less than the rest of His Majesty's subjects in the Province.'

Towards the Indians Lawrence adopted the same tone as towards the Acadians. The tribes at Cape Sable had for some time talked of peace, and an alliance with them was particularly to be encouraged. The French were becoming more of a menace, having strengthened their works at 'Baye Verte and Beausejour, between which places they lately have made a very fine road and continue to seduce our French inhabitants to go over to them.' The message, however, which Lawrence sent to the Indians was hardly calculated to produce the desired results.

'In short if the Indians,' the message ran, 'or he [Le Loutre] on their behalf, have anything to propose of this kind about which they are really in earnest, they very well know where and how to apply.'[51]

The answer of the Indians was communicated by Le Loutre. They agreed to offer no insult to the English who kept to the highway, but they promised to treat as enemies all those who departed from it. If a durable peace was to be made, they demanded the cession to them of an exclusive territory suitable for hunting and fishing and for a mission. This territory was to extend from Baie Verte through Cobequid (Truro) to the Shubenacadie, along the south coast to the peninsula of Canso, and back to Baie Verte—an area comprising half the province of Nova Scotia. Whether the Indians were serious in their application for this immense domain, we know not; probably it was an answer to the haughty note of Lawrence. Considering the demand of the Indians insolent, the Council at Halifax vouchsafed no reply to it; but the commandant of Fort Lawrence at Chignecto was instructed to inform the Indians 'that if they have any serious thoughts of making peace…they may repair to Halifax,' where any reasonable proposal would be considered.

A case instructive of the new temper of the administration was that of the Abbe Daudin of Pisiquid. The abbe had been suspected of stirring up trouble among the Indians, and Captain Murray of Fort Edward was requested to keep an eye on him. When the inhabitants refused to bring in wood for fuel and for the repair of the fort, as they had been ordered to do, and presented to Murray a statement signed by eighty-six of their people, declaring that their oath of fidelity did not require them to furnish the garrison with wood, Murray attributed their conduct to the influence of Daudin. Murray therefore received instructions to repeat his orders, and to summon Daudin and five others to appear at Halifax under pain of arrest. When questioned by Murray, Daudin took the ground that the people, who were free, should have been contracted with, and not treated as slaves; but he asserted that if Murray had consulted

[51] Nova Scotia Documents, p. 210.

him instead of reporting to Lawrence, he could have brought the inhabitants to him in a submissive manner. When requested to repair to Halifax, Daudin pleaded illness; and his followers became insolent, and questioned Murray's authority. Daudin and five others were immediately arrested and sent under escort to the capital.

At a special meeting of the Council held on the evening of October 2, 1754, Claude Brossart, Charles Le Blanc, Baptiste Galerne, and Joseph Hebert were required to explain their refusal to obey the orders of Murray, and the following examination took place:

Q. Why did you not comply with that order to bring in firewood?

A. Some of them had wood and some had not, therefore they gave in the remonstrance to Captain Murray.

Q. Why was that not represented in the remonstrance, which contained an absolute refusal without setting forth any cause?

A. They did not understand the contents of it.

Q. Was the proclamation ever published at the church and stuck up against the wall, and by whom?

A. It was, and they believe by John Hebert.

Q. Was it put up with the wrong side uppermost?

A. They heard that it was.

The inhabitants were never known to boast of a reckless facility in reading, even under normal conditions, and no doubt the grotesque appearance of the letters in the inverted document prompted the answer that 'they did not understand the contents of it.' Neither have we any evidence to prove that John Hebert contributed to their enlightenment by reading the document. The prisoners, however, were severely reprimanded by the Council, and were ordered under pain of military execution to bring in the firewood.

The Abbe Daudin, when brought before the Council, was questioned as to his position in the province. He replied that he served 'only as a simple missionary to occupy himself in spiritual affairs; not in temporal.' The abbe denied that he had made the statements attributed to him, and was allowed to prepare a paper which he termed his defence. The next day his defence was presented and read; but the Council considered that it did not contain anything 'material towards his justification' and ordered his removal from the province. A few weeks later, however, the inhabitants addressed a communication to Lawrence, asking for the reinstatement of the abbe. They expressed their submission to the government, promising to comply with the order regarding the supply of wood; and the Council, considering that the Acadians could not obtain another priest, relented and permitted the abbe to return to his duties.

It is noteworthy, however, that Lawrence's regime was not so rigorous as to prevent some of the Acadians who had abandoned their lands and emigrated to French territory from returning to Nova Scotia. In October 1754 six families, consisting of twenty-eight persons who had settled in Cape Breton, returned to Halifax in a destitute condition. They declared that they had been terrified by the threats of Le Loutre, and by the picture he had drawn of the fate that would befall them at the hands of the Indians if they remained under the domination of the English; that they had retired to Cape Breton, where they had remained ever since; but that the lands given them had been unproductive, and that they had been unable to support their families. They therefore wished to return to their former habitations. They cheerfully subscribed to the oath which was tendered them, and in consideration of their poverty twenty-four of them were allowed provisions during the winter, and the other four a week's provisions 'to subsist them till they returned to their former habitations at Pisiquid.' The Council considered that their return would have a good effect. Thus it came about that the pangs of hunger accomplished a result which threats and promises had failed to produce.

While Lawrence was formulating his policy with regard to the Acadians, events were at the same time rapidly moving towards a renewal of war between France and Great Britain in North America. Indeed, though as yet there had been no formal declaration, the American phase of the momentous Seven Years' War had already begun. France had been dreaming of a colonial empire stretching from Newfoundland to the Gulf of Mexico. She had asserted her ownership of the valleys of the Ohio and the Mississippi; and she had set before herself the object of confining the English colonies within limits as narrow as possible. In May 1754 Shirley, the governor of Massachusetts, had advised the home government that he had received intelligence from Halifax 'that some of the rebel inhabitants of Chignecto, together with the Indians of the Peninsula and St John River, are through the influence of the French garrison at Beausejour engaged in an enterprise to break up all the eastern settlements,' and he pointed out that 'if the advices are true, they will afford...one instance of the many mischievous consequences to the colonists of New England as well as to His Majesty's Province of Nova Scotia which must proceed from the French of Canada having possessed themselves of the isthmus of the Peninsula and St John's river in the Bay of Fundy, and continuing their encroachments within His Majesty's territories.'[52] To this communication the government had replied in July 1754 that it was the king's wish that Shirley should co-operate with Lawrence in attacking the French forts in Nova Scotia.

The British, therefore, determined upon aggressive action. In December Shirley acknowledged having received certain proposals made by Lawrence 'for driving the French of Canada out of Nova Scotia according to the scheme laid down in your letters to me and instructions to Colonel Monckton. I viewed this plan most justly calculated by Your Honour for His Majesty's Service with great pleasure and did not hesitate to

---

[52] Nova Scotia Documents, p. 382. Shirley to Sir T. Robinson, May 23, 1754.

send you the assistance you desir'd of me for carrying it into execution, as soon as I had perused it....I came to a determination to co-operate with you in the most vigorous manner, for effecting the important service within your own Government, which Your Honour may depend upon my prosecuting to the utmost of my power.'[53] In a letter to the Lords of Trade in January 1755, Lawrence expressed the opinion that 'no measure I could take for the security of the Province would have the desired effect until the fort at Beausejour and every French settlement on the north side of the Bay of Fundy was absolutely extirpated, having very good intelligence that the French had determined as soon as ever they had put the fortifications of Louisbourg into a tolerable condition to make themselves masters of the Bay of Fundy by taking our fort at Chignecto.'[54]

In accordance with this Colonel Monckton was instructed to prepare for an expedition against Beausejour and St John in the spring of 1755. He was given for the purpose a letter of unlimited credit on Boston; and every regiment in Nova Scotia was brought up to the strength of one thousand men. By May the expedition was ready. Monckton, with two thousand troops, embarked at Annapolis Royal, and by June 1 the expedition was at Chignecto. In the meantime Vergor, the French commandant at Beausejour, had not been passive. He had strengthened his defences, had summoned the inhabitants of the surrounding districts to his help, had mounted cannon in a blockhouse defending the passage of the river, and had thrown up a strong breastwork of timber along the shore. On June 3 the British landed. They had little difficulty in driving the French from their entrenchments. The inhabitants had no heart in the work of defence; and the French, unable to make a stand, threw their cannon into the river and burned the blockhouse and other buildings. They then retired to the fort, together with about two hundred and twenty of the Acadians; the rest of the

---

[53] Nova Scotia Documents, p. 389. Shirley says: 'It is now near eleven at night and I have been writing hard since seven in the morning...and can scarce hold the pen in my hand.'
[54] Lawrence to Lords of Trade, January 12, 1755.

Acadians threw away their arms and ammunition, asserting that they did not wish to be hanged. The British took up a position in the woods about a mile and a half from the fort; and on the 13th they succeeded in establishing a battery on a hill within easy range. The bombardment of the place, which began the next day, was at first ineffective; and for a time the British were driven back. But, in the meantime, news reached the French that no reinforcements could be expected from Louisbourg; and such disaffection arose among the Acadians that they were forbidden by a council of war to deliberate together or to desert the fort under pain of being shot. When the British renewed the attack, however, the Acadians requested Vergor to capitulate; and he feebly acquiesced. The British offered very favourable terms. So far as the Acadians were concerned, it was proposed that, since they had taken up arms under threat of death, they were to be pardoned and allowed to return to their homes and enjoy the free exercise of their religion. The soldiers of the garrison were sent as prisoners to Halifax.

After the fall of Beausejour, which Monckton renamed Fort Cumberland, the British met with little further resistance. Fort Gaspereau on Baie Verte, against which Monckton next proceeded, was evacuated by the commandant Villeray, who found himself unable to obtain the assistance of the Acadians. And the few Acadians at the river St John, when Captain Rous appeared before the settlement with three ships, made an immediate submission. Rous destroyed the cannon, burned the fort, and retired with his troops up the river. The Indians of the St John, evidently impressed by the completeness of the British success and awed by their strong force, invited Rous to come ashore, and assured him of their friendliness.

Having removed the menace of the French forts, Lawrence was now able to deal more freely with the question of the Acadians. The opportunity for action was not long in presenting itself. In June the Acadians of Minas presented to Lawrence a petition couched in language not as tactful as it might have been. In this memorial they requested the restoration of some of their former privileges. They first assured the lieutenant-governor of their fidelity, which they had maintained in face of threats on the part of the French, and of their determination to remain loyal when in the enjoyment of former liberties. They asked to be allowed the use of their canoes, a privilege of which they were deprived on the pretext that they had been carrying provisions to the French at Beausejour. Some refugees might have done so, but they had not. They used these canoes for fishing to maintain their families. By an order of June 4 they had been required to hand in their guns. Some of them had done so, but they needed them for protection against the wild beasts, which were more numerous since the Indians had left these parts. The possession of a gun did not induce them to rebel, neither did the withdrawal of the weapon render them more faithful. Loyalty was a matter of conscience. If they decided to remain faithful, they wished to know what were the lieutenant-governor's intentions towards them.

On receiving this memorial Lawrence ordered the deputies of the Acadians to remain in Halifax, on the ground that the paper was impertinent. Upon this the deputies presented another memorial, in which they disclaimed any intention of disrespect, and wished to be allowed a hearing in order to explain. The Council held a meeting; and the lieutenant-governor explained 'that Captain Murray had informed him that for some time before the delivery of the first of the said memorials the French inhabitants in general had behaved with greater submission and obedience to the orders of Government than usual, and had already delivered to him a considerable number of their firearms; but that at the delivery of the said memorial they treated him with great indecency and insolence, which gave him strong suspicions that they had obtained some intelligence which we were then ignorant of, and which the lieutenant-governor conceived might most probably be a report that had been about that time spread amongst them of a French fleet being then in the Bay of Fundy.'[55] The deputies were then brought in and told that if they had not submitted the second memorial they would have been punished for their presumption. 'They were severely reprimanded for their audacity in subscribing and presenting so impertinent a paper,

---

[55] Minutes of Council, July 3, 1755.

but in compassion to their weakness and ignorance of the nature of our constitution,' the Council professed itself still ready to treat them with leniency, and ordered the memorial to be read paragraph by paragraph.

When the question of the oath came up for discussion, the deputies said they were ready to take it as they had done before. To this the Council replied that 'His Majesty had disapproved of the manner of their taking the oath before' and 'that it was not consistent with his honour to make any conditions.' The deputies were then allowed until the following morning to come to a resolution. On the next day they declared that they could not consent to take the oath in the form required without consulting others. They were then informed that as the taking of the oath was a personal act and as they had for themselves refused to take it as directed by law, and had therefore sufficiently evinced the sincerity of their unfriendliness towards the government, the Council could look upon them no longer as subjects of His Majesty, but must treat them hereafter as subjects of the king of France. They were ordered to withdraw. The Council then decided that with regard to the oath none of them should for the future be admitted to take it after having once refused to do so, but that effectual measures ought to be taken to remove all such recusants out of the province. The deputies, again being called in and informed of this resolution, offered to take the oath, but were informed that there was no reason to hope that 'their proposed compliance proceeds from an honest mind and can be esteemed only the effect of compulsion and force, and is contrary to a clause in 1 Geo. II, c. 13, whereby persons who have once refused to take oaths cannot be afterwards permitted to take them, but are considered as Popish recusants.' Therefore they could not be indulged with such permission. Later they were ordered into confinement.

On the 25th of July a memorial signed by over two hundred of the inhabitants of Annapolis Royal was laid before the Council. The memorialists said they had unanimously consented to deliver up their firearms, although they had never had any desire to use them against His Majesty's government. They declared that they had nothing to reproach themselves with, for they had always been loyal, and that several of them had risked their lives in order to give information regarding the enemy. They would abide by the old oath, but they could not take a new one. The deputies who had brought this memorial from Annapolis, on being called before the Council and asked what they had to say regarding the new oath, declared 'that they could not take any other oath than what they had formerly taken.' If it was the king's intention, they added, to force them out of the country, they hoped 'that they should be allowed a convenient time for their departure.' The Council warned them of the consequences of their refusal; and they were allowed until the following Monday to decide. Their final answer was polite, but obdurate:

> Inasmuch as a report is in circulation among us, the French inhabitants of this province, that His Excellency the Governor demands of us an oath of obedience conformable, in some manner, to that of natural subjects of His Majesty King George the Second, and as, in consequence, we are morally certain that several of our inhabitants are detained and put to inconvenience at Halifax for that object; if the above are his intentions with respect to us, we all take the liberty of representing to His Excellency, and to all the inhabitants, that we and our fathers, having taken an oath of fidelity, which has been approved of several times in the name of the King, and under the privileges of which we have lived faithful and obedient, and protected by His Majesty the King of Great Britain, according to the letters and proclamation of His Excellency Governor Shirley, dated 16th of September 1746, and 21st of October 1747, we will never prove so fickle as to take an oath which changes, ever so little, the conditions and the privileges obtained for us by our sovereign and our fathers in the past.

> And as we are well aware that the King, our master, loves and protects only constant, faithful, and free subjects, and as it is only by virtue of his kindness, and

of the fidelity which we have always preserved towards His Majesty, that he has granted to us, and that he still continues to grant to us, the entire possession of our property and the free and public exercise of the Roman Catholic Religion, we desire to continue, to the utmost of our power, to be faithful and dutiful in the same manner that we were allowed to be by His Excellency Mr Richard Philipps.

Charity for our detained inhabitants, and their innocence, obliged us to beg Your Excellency, to allow yourself to be touched by their miseries, and to restore to them that liberty which we ask for them, with all possible submission and the most profound respect.

The inhabitants of Pisiquid presented a similar petition. They hoped that they would be listened to, and that the imprisoned deputies would be released. Another memorial was presented by the inhabitants of Minas. They refused to take a new oath; and thereupon their deputies were ordered to be imprisoned.

There was now, the Council considered, only one course left open for it to pursue. Nothing remained but to consider the means which should be taken to send the inhabitants out of the province, and distribute them among the several colonies on the continent.

'I am determined,' Lawrence had written, 'to bring the inhabitants to a compliance, or rid the province of such perfidious subjects.'[56] He was now about to fulfil his promise.

---

[56] Lawrence to Lords of Trade, July 18, 1755.

CHAPTER IX

THE EXPULSION

The imprisonment of the deputies, on George's Island at Halifax, naturally agitated the minds of the simple Acadians. In the ripening fields and in the villages might be seen groups discussing the fate of their companions. But, though they may have feared further punitive acts at the hands of the British, they were totally unprepared for the approaching catastrophe, and did not for a moment dream that they were to be cast out of their homes, deprived of all they held dear in the land of their nativity, and sent adrift as wanderers and exiles.

It is no part of this narrative to sit in judgment or to debate whether the forcible expatriation of the Acadians was a necessary measure or a justifiable act of war. However this may be, it is important to fix the responsibility for a deed so painful in its execution and so momentous in its consequences.

The Council at Halifax had no power to enact laws. Its action was limited to the authority vested in the governor by his commission and his instructions. And, as Lawrence had as yet neither commission nor instructions,[57] he asked the chief justice, Jonathan Belcher, to prepare an opinion, as he desired to be fortified with legal authority for the drastic act on which he had determined. Belcher had arrived in Nova Scotia from New England nine months before. He does not appear to have examined the official correspondence between the years 1713 and 1755, or even the Minutes of Council. At any rate, he presented a document ill-founded in fact and contemptible in argument. The Acadians are not to be allowed to remain, he said, because 'it will be contrary to the letter and spirit of His Majesty's instructions to Governor Cornwallis, and in my humble apprehension would incur the displeasure of the crown

---

[57] He had not yet been appointed governor. Hopson had wished to resign in the summer of 1754; but the Lords of Trade, who held him in high esteem, had refused to accept his resignation, and Lawrence had been made merely lieutenant-governor, though with the full salary of a governor.

and the parliament.'[58] What the instructions to Cornwallis had to do with it is not clear. There is no clause in that document contemplating the forcible removal of the people. But even this is immaterial, since the instructions to Cornwallis were not then in force. Hopson, who had succeeded Cornwallis, had been given new instructions, and the Council was governed by them, since, legally at any rate, Hopson was still governor in 1755; and, according to his instructions, Hopson was 'to issue a declaration in His Majesty's name setting forth, that tho' His Majesty is fully sensible that the many indulgences...to the said inhabitants in allowing them the entirely free exercise of their religion and the quiet peaceable possession of their lands, have not met with a dutiful return, but on the contrary, divers of the said inhabitants have openly abetted or privately assisted His Majesty's enemies...yet His Majesty being desirous of shewing marks of his royal grace to the said inhabitants, in hopes thereby to induce them to become for the future true and loyal subjects, is pleased to declare, that the said inhabitants shall continue in the free exercise of their religion, as far as the Laws of Great Britain shall admit of the same...provided that the said inhabitants do within three months from the date of such declaration...take the Oath of Allegiance.' The next clause instructed the governor to report to the Lords of Trade on the effect of the declaration. If the inhabitants or any part of them should refuse the oath, he was to ascertain 'His Majesty's further directions in what manner to conduct yourself towards such of the French inhabitants as shall not have complied therewith.'[59] Hopson had tendered the oath to the Acadians. The oath had been refused by them. Their refusal had been reported to the government; and there the matter rested.

In another paragraph of the opinion the chief justice asserted that 'persons are declared recusants if they refuse on a summons to take the oath at the sessions, and can never after such refusal be permitted to take them.' This, no doubt, was the

---

[58] Public Archives, Canada. Nova Scotia A, vol. lviii, p. 380. Opinion of Chief Justice Belcher.
[59] Public Archives, Canada. Nova Scotia E, vol. ii. Instructions to Governors.

law. But the king had ignored the law, and had commanded his representatives in Nova Scotia to tender the oath again to a people who, upon several occasions, had refused to take it. It was not reasonable, therefore, to suppose, as the chief justice did, that the king would be displeased at the performance of an act which he had expressly commanded.

We have seen that, in the spring of 1754, when Lawrence had intimated to the government that a number of the Acadians who had gone over to the enemy were now anxious to return to their lands, which he would not permit until they had taken an oath without reserve, he was advised not to 'create a diffidence in their minds which might induce them to quit the province.' That this was still the policy is evident from a letter to the same effect written to Lawrence by Sir Thomas Robinson of the British ministry on August 13, 1755, two weeks after the ominous decision of the Halifax Council.[60] Lawrence, however, could not have received this last communication until the plans for the expulsion were well advanced. On the other hand, the decision of the Council was not received in England until November 20, so that the king was not aware of it until the expulsion was already a reality. The meaning of these facts is clear. The thing was done by Lawrence and his Council without the authority or knowledge of the home government.[61]

The proceedings in connection with the expulsion were carried on simultaneously in different parts of the province; and

---

[60] Nova Scotia Documents, p. 279. Here is a sentence from the letter: 'It cannot therefore be too much recommended to you, to use the greatest caution and prudence in your conduct towards these neutrals, and to assure such of them as may be trusted, especially upon their taking the oaths to His Majesty and his government, that they may remain in the quiet possession of their settlements, under proper regulations.'

[61] At the meeting of the Halifax Council which decreed the removal of the Acadians the following members were present: the lieutenant-governor, Benjamin Green, John Collier, William Cotterell, John Rous, and Jonathan Belcher. Vice-Admiral Boscawen and Rear-Admiral Mostyn were also present at the 'earnest request' of the Council.—Minutes of Council, July 28, 1755.

the circumstances varied according to the temper or situation of the people. It will be convenient to deal with each group or district separately.

On July 31, 1755, Lawrence ordered Colonel Monckton, who lay with his troops at the newly captured Fort Cumberland, to gather in the inhabitants of the isthmus of Chignecto, and of Chepody, on the north shore of the Bay. The district of Minas was committed to the care of Colonel Winslow. Captain Murray, in command at Fort Edward, was to secure the inhabitants of Pisiquid, and Major Handfield, at Annapolis Royal, the people in his district.

It is regrettable that we do not find in the instructions to these officers any discrimination made between the Acadians who had persistently refused to take the oath and those who had been recognized by the governor and Council as British subjects. Monckton was advised to observe secrecy, and to 'endeavour to fall upon some stratagem to get the men, both young and old (especially the heads of families)' into his power, and to detain them until the transports should arrive. He was also to inform the inhabitants that all their cattle and corn were now the property of the crown, and no person should be allowed to carry off 'the least thing but their ready money and household furniture.'[62] On August 8 Monckton was advised that the transports would be available soon, and that in the interval he would do well to destroy all the villages in the vicinity of Beausejour or Cumberland, and to use 'every other method to distress as much as can be, those who may attempt to conceal themselves in the woods.' Monckton promptly conceived a plan to entrap the people. He issued a summons, calling upon the adult males to appear at Fort Cumberland on the 11th. About four hundred responded to the call. The proceedings were summary. Monckton merely told them that by the decision of the Council they were declared rebels on account of their past misdeeds; that their lands and chattels were forfeited to the crown, and that in the meantime they

---

[62] Nova Scotia Documents, p. 267.

would be treated as prisoners.[63] The gates of the fort were then closed.

Less successful was Captain Cobb, who had been sent to Chepody to capture the Acadians there. Before his arrival the people had fled to the woods. Three other parties, detached from Fort Cumberland to scour the country in search of stragglers, reported various successes. Major Preble returned the next day with three Acadians, and Captain Perry brought in eleven. Captain Lewis, who had gone to Cobequid, had captured two vessels bound for Louisbourg with cattle and sheep, and had taken several prisoners and destroyed a number of villages on the route.

The more energetic of the Acadians still at large were not easily caught. The pangs of hunger, however, might tempt many to leave the security of their hiding-places, and Monckton determined to gather in as many more as possible. On August 28 Captain Frye sailed from Fort Cumberland for Chepody, Memramcook, and Petitcodiac, on the north shore, with orders to take prisoners and burn the villages on the way.[64] Captain Gilbert was sent to Baie Verte on a similar mission. Finding the village deserted on his arrival at Chepody, Frye set fire to the buildings and sailed toward Petitcodiac. On the way the appearance of a house or a barn seems to have been the signal for the vessels to cast anchor, while a party of soldiers, torch in hand, laid waste the homes of the peasantry. On September 4, however, the expedition suffered a serious check. A landing party of about sixty were applying the torch to a village on the shore, when they were set upon by a hundred Indians and Acadians, and a general engagement ensued. The British, though reinforced by men from the ships, were severely handled; and in the end Frye regained the boats with a loss of twenty-three killed and missing and eleven wounded. This

[63] Collections of the Nova Scotia Historical Society, vol. iv, Journal of Colonel John Winslow, part i, p. 227.

[64] 'Major Frye with a party of 200 men embarked on Board Captain Cobb Newel and Adams to go to Sheperday and take what French thay Could and burn thare vilges thare and at Petcojack.'—Collections of the Nova Scotia Historical Society, vol. i, p. 131. Diary of John Thomas.

attack was the work of Boishebert, the Canadian leader, whom we met some time ago at St John. On the capture of that place by Rous in the summer Boishebert had taken to the woods with his followers, and was assisting the settlers of Chepody to gather in the harvest when Frye's raiders appeared. Frye did not attempt to pursue his assailants, but retired at once to Fort Cumberland with twenty-three captured women and children. He had, however, destroyed over two hundred buildings and a large quantity of wheat and flax. Meanwhile Gilbert had laid waste the village at Baie Verte and the neighbouring farms.[65]

By August 31 the transports had arrived at Beausejour, and early in the month of September the embarkation began. The work, however, was tedious, and in the interval the English met with another misfortune. On October 1 eighty-six Acadian prisoners dug a hole under the wall of Fort Lawrence and, eluding the vigilance of the guards, made good their escape in the night.[66] But on October 13 a fleet of ten sail, carrying nine hundred and sixty Acadian exiles, left Chignecto Bay bound for South Carolina and Georgia. After the departure of the vessels the soldiers destroyed every barn and house in the vicinity and drove several herds of cattle into Fort Cumberland.[67]

Lawrence was now rid of nearly a thousand Acadians. It was less than he expected, to be sure, and yet no doubt it was a great relief to him. About this time he should have received Sir Thomas Robinson's letter of August 13, conveying to him the king's wishes in effect that the Acadians were not to be

---

[65] 'A Party Likewise from ye Bay of verte under ye comand of Capt. Gilbert who had bin and consumed that vilige and the Houses adjasent.'—Diary of John Thomas.

[66] 'Stormy Dark Night Eighty Six French Prisoners Dugg under ye Wall att Foart Lawrance and got Clear undiscovered by ye Centry.'—Diary of John Thomas.

[67] We Burnt 30 Houses Brought away one Woman 200 Hed of Neat Cattle 20 Horses...we mustered about Sunrise mustered the Cattle Togather Drove them over ye River near westcock Sot Near 50 Houses on Fyre and Returned to Fort Cumberland with our Cattle etc. about 6 Clock P.M.'—Diary of John Thomas, pp. 136-7.

molested.[68] This letter received in time would no doubt have stopped the whole undertaking. But now that some of the people had already been deported, there was nothing to be done but to go on with the business to the bitter end.

At Annapolis Royal, more than a hundred miles south of Monckton's camp, matters proceeded more slowly. Handfield, the commandant there, had decided to wait for the arrival of the promised transports before attempting to round up the inhabitants. Then, when his soldiers went forward on their mission up the river, no sound of human voice met their ears in any of the settlements. The inhabitants had hidden in the woods. Handfield appealed to Winslow, who was then at Grand Pre, for more troops to bring the people to reason.[69] But Winslow had no troops to spare. Handfield does not appear to have relished his task, which he described as a 'disagreeable and troublesome part of the service.' What induced the inhabitants to return to their homes is not clear, but early in the month of September they resumed their occupations. They remained unmolested until early in November, when a fresh detachment of troops arrived to assist in their removal. On December 4 over sixteen hundred men, women, and children were crowded into the transports, which lay off Goat Island and which four days later set sail at eight o'clock in the morning.

Meanwhile Captain Murray of Fort Edward was doing his duty in the Pisiquid neighbourhood. On September 5 he wrote to Winslow at Grand Pre, only a few miles distant: 'I have succeeded finely and have got 183 men into my possession.'[70] But there was still much to be done. Three days later he wrote again: 'I am afraid there will be some lives lost before they are got together, for you know our soldiers hate them, and if they can find a pretence to kill them, they will.' Of the means Murray employed to accomplish his task we are not told, but he

---

[68] The date of the receipt of this letter is uncertain; but it is evident that he received it before the 30th of November, as on that day he replied to a letter of the 13th of August.

[69] Winslow's Journal, part ii, p. 96.

[70] Winslow's Journal, part ii, p. 96.

must have been exceedingly active up to October 14, for on that date nine hundred persons had been gathered into his net. His real troubles now began; he was short of provisions and without transports. At last two arrived, one of ninety tons, and the other of one hundred and fifty: these, however, would not accommodate half the people. Another sloop was promised, but it was slow in coming. He became alarmed. 'Good God, what can keep her!' he wrote. 'I earnestly entreat you to send her with all despatch... Then with the three sloops and more vessels I will put them aboard, let the consequence be what it will.'[71] He was as good as his word. On October 23 Winslow wrote: 'Captain Murray has come from Pisiquid with upwards of one thousand people in four vessels.'[72]

Colonel Winslow arrived on August 19 at Grand Pre, in the district of Minas. After requesting the inhabitants to remove all sacred objects from the church, which he intended to use as a place of arms, he took up his quarters in the presbytery. A camp was then formed around the church, and enclosed by a picket-fence. His first action was to summon the principal inhabitants to inform them that they would be required to furnish provisions for the troops during their occupancy, and to take effective measures to protect the crops which had not yet been garnered. There was danger that if the object of his visit were to become known, the grain might be destroyed. He was careful, therefore, to see that the harvest was gathered in before making any unfavourable announcement.

On August 29 Winslow held a consultation with Murray as to the most expeditious means of effecting the removal of the people. The next day three sloops from Boston came to anchor in the basin. There was, of course, immediate and intense excitement among the inhabitants; yet, in spite of all inquiries regarding their presence, no information could be elicited from either the crews or the soldiers. On September 2, however, Winslow issued a proclamation informing the people that the lieutenant- governor had a communication to impart to them respecting a new resolution, and that His Majesty's intentions in

---

[71] Ibid., p. 173.
[72] Ibid., p. 178.

respect thereto would be made known. They were, therefore, to appear in the church at Grand Pre on Friday, September 5, at three o'clock in the afternoon. No excuse would be accepted for non-attendance; and should any fail to attend, their lands and chattels would be forfeited to the crown.

Winslow's position was by no means strong. He had taken all the precautions possible; but he was short of provisions, and there was no sign of the expected supply-ship, the Saul. Besides, the Acadians far outnumbered his soldiers, and should they prove rebellious trouble might ensue. 'Things are now very heavy on my heart and hands,' he wrote a few days later. 'I wish we had more men, but as it is shall I question not to be able to scuffle through.'[73]

The eventful 5th of September arrived, and at three o'clock four hundred and eighteen of the inhabitants walked slowly into the church, which had been familiar to them from their youth, and closely connected with the most solemn as well as with the most joyous events of their lives. Here their children had been baptized, and here many of them had been united in the bonds of matrimony. Here the remains of those they loved had been carried, ere they were consigned to their final resting-place, and here, too, after divine service, they had congregated to glean intelligence of what was going on in the world beyond their ken. Now, however, the scene was changed. Guards were at the door; and in the centre of the church a table had been placed, round which soldiers were drawn up. Presently Colonel Winslow entered, attended by his officers. Deep silence fell upon the people as he began to speak. The substance of his speech has been preserved in his Journal, as follows:

Gentlemen, I have received from His Excellency, Governor Lawrence, the King's commission which I have in my hand. By his orders you are convened to hear His Majesty's final resolution in respect to the French inhabitants of this his province of Nova Scotia, who for almost half a century have had more indulgence granted them than any of his subjects in any

---

[73] Winslow's Journal, part ii, p. 97.

part of his dominions. What use you have made of it, you yourselves best know.

The duty I am now upon, though necessary, is very disagreeable to my natural make and temper, as I know it must be grievous to you who are of the same species. But it is not my business to animadvert, but to obey such orders as I receive; and therefore without hesitation I shall deliver you His Majesty's orders and instructions, namely: That your lands and tenements, cattle of all kinds and live stock of all sorts are forfeited to the Crown with all your other effects, saving your money and household goods, and that you yourselves are to be removed from this his province.

Thus it is peremptorily His Majesty's orders that all the French inhabitants of these districts be removed; and through His Majesty's goodness I am directed to allow you liberty to carry with you your money and as many of your household goods as you can take without discommoding the vessels you go in. I shall do everything in my power that all these goods be secured to you, and that you be not molested in carrying them with you, and also that whole families shall go in the samevessel; so that this removal which I am sensible must give you a great deal of trouble may be made as easy as His Majesty's service will admit; and I hope that in whatever part of the world your lot may fall, you may be faithful subjects, and a peaceable and happy people.

I must also inform you that it is His Majesty's pleasure that you remain in security under the inspection and direction of the troops that I have the honour to command.[74]

---

[74] Winslow's Journal, part ii, p. 94. It is not thought necessary here to follow the grotesque spelling of the original. It will be noted that the doom of the people is pronounced in the name of the king. But, as

This address having been delivered and interpreted to the people, Winslow issued orders to the troops and seamen not to kill any of the cattle or rob the orchards, as the lands and possessions of the inhabitants were now the property of the king. He then withdrew to his quarters in the presbytery, leaving the soldiers on guard.

The first thoughts of the stricken prisoners were of their families, with whom they had no means of communication and who would not understand the cause of their detention. After some conversation together, a few of the elders asked leave to speak to the commander. This being granted, they requested to be allowed to carry the melancholy news to the homes of the prisoners. Winslow at length ordered them to choose each day twenty men, for whom the others would be held responsible, to communicate with their families, and to bring in food for all the prisoners.

Only five transports lay in the basin of Minas. No provisions were in sight. It was impossible as yet to put all the prisoners on board. More had been captured, and they now outnumbered Winslow's troops nearly two to one. Presently news came of the disaster to Frye's party at Chepody. Winslow, having observed suspicious movements among the prisoners, began to fear for the safety of his own position. He held a consultation with his officers. It was decided to divide the prisoners, and put fifty of the younger men on each of the transports.[75] The parish priest, Father Landry, who had a good knowledge of English and was the principal spokesman of the Acadians, was told to inform the inhabitants that one hour would be given them to prepare for going on board. Winslow then brought up the whole of his troops, and stationed them between the door of the church and the gate. The Acadians

---

already stated, the king or the home government knew nothing of it; and instructions of a quite contrary tenor were even then on their way to Lawrence.

[75] Winslow's Journal, part ii, p. 108.—'September 10. Called my officers together and communicated to them what I had observed, and after debating matters it was determined, 'nemine contradicente', that it would be best to divide the prisoners.'

were drawn up; the young men were told off and ordered to march. They refused to obey unless their fathers might accompany them.[76] Winslow informed them that orders were orders, that this was not the time for parley, and commanded the troops to fix bayonets and advance. This appears to have had the effect desired, for, with the assistance of the commander, who pushed one of them along, twenty-four men started off and the rest followed. The road from the church to the ships, nearly a mile and a half in length, was lined by hundreds of women and children, who fell on their knees weeping and praying. Eighty soldiers conducted the procession, which moved but slowly. Some of the men sang, some wept, and others prayed.[77] At last the young men were put aboard and left under guard, while the escort returned to bring another contingent of the prisoners; and so until all who were deemed dangerous had been disposed of. The vessels had not been provisioned; but the women and children brought daily to the shore food which the soldiers conveyed to the prisoners.

After this it appears that the soldiers committed some depredations in the neighbourhood, and Winslow issued an order forbidding any one to leave the camp after the roll-call.[78] In the meantime parties were sent to remote parts of the rivers

---

[76] Ibid., p. 109.—'They all answered they would not go without their fathers. I told them that was a word I did not understand, for that the King's command was to me absolute and should be absolutely obeyed, and that I did not love to use harsh means, but that the time did not admit of parleys or delays; and then ordered the whole troops to fix their bayonets and advance towards the French. I bid the four right-hand files of the prisoners, consisting of twenty-four men, which I told off myself to divide from the rest, one of whom I took hold on.'

[77] Winslow's Journal, part ii, p. 109.—'They went off praying, singing, and crying, being met by the women and children all the way (which is a mile and a half), with great lamentations.'

[78] Winslow's Journal, part ii, p. 113.—'September 13. No party or person will be permitted to go out after calling the roll on any account whatever, as many bad things have been done lately in the night, to the distressing of the distressed French inhabitants in this neighbourhood.'

in search of stragglers, but only thirty, very old and infirm, were found, and it was decided to leave them ashore until the ships should be ready to depart. It still remained, however, to bring in the inhabitants of the parish of Cobequid, and a detachment under Captain Lewis was dispatched on this errand. He returned without a prisoner. The inhabitants of Cobequid had fled; but Lewis reported that he had laid their habitations in ruins.

Neither the needed transports nor the provisions had arrived. Winslow chafed and groaned. He longed to be rid of the painful and miserable business. At last, on the evening of September 28, came the belated supply-ship; but where were the transports? Winslow resolved to fill up the five vessels which lay in the basin, and ordered that the women and children should be brought to the shore. Families and those of the same village were to be kept together, as far as possible.

Meanwhile twenty-four of the young men imprisoned on the ships made good their escape, and one Francois Hebert was charged as an abettor. Winslow ordered Hebert to be brought ashore, and, to impress upon the Acadians the gravity of his offence, his house and barn were set on fire in his presence. At the same time the inhabitants were warned that unless the young men surrendered within two days all their household furniture would be confiscated and their habitations destroyed. If captured, no quarter would be given them. The result was that twenty-two of the young men returned to the transports. The other two were overtaken by the soldiers and shot.[79]

Finally a number of transports arrived, and, on October 8, amid scenes of wild confusion, the embarkation began in earnest. From the villages far and near came the families of those who were detained in the church and on the vessels. Some came aiding the infirm or carrying the sick, while others were laden with bundles of their personal effects. Most were on foot, although a few rode in the vehicles bringing their household goods. Old and young wended their way to the vessels, weary and footsore and sad at heart. In all, eighty families were taken to the boats. The next day the men who

---

[79] Winslow's Journal, part ii, p. 173.

had been imprisoned on the vessels since September 10 were brought ashore in order that they might join their families and accompany the people of their own villages. Four days later (October 13) several of the ships received sailing orders, some for Maryland, others for Pennsylvania, and others for Virginia.

By the 1st of November Winslow had sent off over fifteen hundred exiles. But his anxieties were by no means at an end. There were still a large number of people to be deported. The difficulty lay in the shortage of transports. After the vessels had been taxed to their utmost, Winslow had still over six hundred persons on his hands;[80] and he was obliged in the meantime to quarter them in houses at Grand Pre. There remained also the task of destroying the villages to prevent their occupation by stragglers, in accordance with Lawrence's orders. Finally, on December 13, transports were provided for the unhappy remnant of the prisoners; and seven days later the last vessels left port. The cruel task was done. In all, over six thousand persons had been forcibly deported, while the rest of the population had been driven to the wilderness and their homes laid waste. Some wandered to the Isle St Jean and others to New Brunswick and Canada. The land of the Acadians was a solitude.

And so, sorrow-framed, the story of the expulsion draws to its close. Hardly had the deplorable work ended, when England made with Frederick of Prussia the treaty which formally inaugurated her Seven Years' War with France. For Lawrence, perhaps, this was a fortunate circumstance. The day of mutual concessions had passed; and an act which a few months before might have been denounced as unwarrantable might now, in the heat of a mighty contest, be regarded as a patriotic service. Nor is this the only instance of the kind in history. Often, indeed, has war served, not only to cover the grossest inhumanities; it has even furnished an excuse for substantial reward.

---

[80] Winslow's Journal, part ii, p. 183.

CHAPTER X

THE EXILES

Thus the Acadians passed from the land of their birth and from the scenes of their youth. Some were to wander as exiles in many lands for many years, separated from their children and from their kind, while others, more fortunate, were soon to regain their native soil.

Lawrence, in his instructions to the governors of the colonies to which he had sent the exiles, said that they were 'to be received and disposed of in such a manner as may best answer our design of preventing their reunion' as a people. It was not intended to tear apart families and friends, but, owing to the scarcity of vessels and the inadequate arrangements for the deportation, there were many cruel separations. The deputies confined since July on George's Island, for example, were at the last moment transferred to Annapolis in order that they might accompany their families, but this was not effected, for the deputies themselves landed in North Carolina, while their wives and children were dispersed in other colonies.[81] One of the leading Acadians, and one who had loyally served the British, Rene Le Blanc, notary of Grand Pre, was landed with his wife and his two youngest children in New York, while his eighteen other children were scattered far and wide.[82] The real separation of families, however, began in the colonies. For example, four hundred persons were transported to Connecticut; but before the whole number arrived an order went forth for their dispersion in fifty towns. Nineteen were allotted to Norwich, while three only were sent to Haddon. In some colonies only the first boats were allowed to disembark the exiles, and the masters of the others were forced to seek other ports.

The treatment of the exiles in the colonies varied according to circumstances. In some instances the younger men and

---

[81] Nova Scotia Documents, p. 280. Calnek and Savary, History of the County of Annapolis, p. 124.

[82] Petition of the Acadians deported to Philadelphia. Printed in Richard, vol. ii, p. 371.

women were bound out to service for periods varying from three to twelve weeks. In others they were left free to maintain themselves by their own efforts, the state to provide for such as were incapable, through age or infirmity, of performing manual labour. Hundreds of those who were placed under control escaped and wandered, footsore and half clad, from town to town in the hope of meeting their relatives or of finding means to return to their former homes. Little record has been preserved of the journeyings of these unfortunates or of the sufferings they endured.

About a third of the people deported from Nova Scotia in 1755 found their way to South Carolina, although that does not appear to have been the destination proposed for them by Lawrence. On November 6, 1755, the South Carolina Gazette announced that 'the Baltimore Snow is expected from the Bay of Fundy with some French Neutrals on board to be distributed in the British colonies.' A fortnight later the first of these arrived, and in the course of a few weeks over a thousand had been landed at Charleston. Soon after, probably passed on by other colonies, a thousand more arrived. Alarmed by the presence of so many strangers, the authorities adopted measures to place them under restraint; and in February 1756 two parties of the prisoners broke loose: thirty of them outdistanced their pursuers; five or six, according to the Gazette, made their way to the plantation of a Mr Williams on the Santee, terrified the family, secured a quantity of clothing and firearms, broke open a box containing money, and headed across the Alleghanies, it was thought, for the French stronghold, Fort Duquesne, where Pittsburgh now stands. This conjecture is probable, since nine Acadians from Fort Duquesne arrived at the river St John some time later. In the interval the South Carolina legislature passed an act for the dispersion of four-fifths of the French Neutrals in various parishes at the public expense, the remaining fifth to be supported at Charleston by the vestry of St Phillips. On April 16 passports were given to one hundred and thirty persons to proceed to Virginia. Here they obtained the authority of the governor to return to Acadia, and they reached the river St John on June 16, 1756. Some time later the governor of South

Carolina gave the remainder of the people permission to go where they pleased. Two old ships and a quantity of inferior provisions were placed at their disposal, and they sailed for Hampton, Virginia. In due course nine hundred of them landed in the district of the river St John, where they were employed by Vaudreuil, the governor of New France, in harrying the British. By the year 1763 only two hundred and eighty-three Acadians remained in South Carolina. One family of the name of Lanneau became Protestants and gave two ministers to the Presbyterian Church—the Rev. John Lanneau, who afterwards went as a missionary to Jerusalem, and the Rev. Basil Lanneau, who became Hebrew tutor in the Theological Seminary at Columbia.

Among the refugees who put out from Minas on October 13, 1755, were some four hundred and fifty destined for Philadelphia. The vessels touched Delaware on November 20, when it was discovered that there were several cases of smallpox on board, and the masters were ordered to leave the shore. They were not permitted to land at Philadelphia until the 10th of December. Many of the exiles died during the winter, and were buried in the cemetery of the poor which now forms a part of Washington Park, Philadelphia. The survivors were lodged in a poor quarter of the town, in 'neutral huts,' as their mean dwellings were termed. When the plague-stricken people arrived, Philadelphia had scarcely recovered from the panic of a recent earthquake. Moreover, there was a letter, said to have been written by Lawrence, dated at Halifax, August 6, and published in the Philadelphia Gazette on September 4, not calculated to place the destitute refugees in a favourable light. This is the substance of the letter: We are now forming the noble project of driving the French Neutrals out of this province. They have long been our secret enemies and have assisted the Indians. If we are able to accomplish their expulsion, it will be one of the great achievements of the English in America, for, among other considerations, the lands which they occupy are among the best in the country, and we can place good English farmers in their stead. A few days later another letter was published to the effect that three Acadians had been arrested charged with poisoning the wells in the vicinity of Halifax. Their trial, it was stated, had not yet taken place; but if guilty they would have but a few hours to live.

Robert Hunter Morris, the governor at this time of Pennsylvania, wrote to Shirley of Massachusetts saying that, as he had not sufficient troops to enforce order, he feared that the Acadians would unite with the Irish and German Catholics in a conspiracy against the state. He also addressed the governor of New Jersey[83] to the same effect. The governor of New Jersey, in his reply, expressed surprise that those who planned to send the French Neutrals, or rather rebels and traitors to the British crown, had not realized that there were already too many strangers for the peace and security of the colonies: that they should have been sent to Old France. He was quite in accord with Morris in believing there was a danger of the people joining the Irish Papists in an attempt to ruin and destroy the king's colonies.

The Acadians had arrived at Philadelphia in a most deplorable condition. One of the Quakers who visited the boats while they were in quarantine reported that they were without shirts and socks and were sadly in need of bed-clothing. A petition to the governor, giving an account of their conduct in Acadia and of the treatment they had received, fell on deaf ears. An act was passed for their dispersion in the counties of Bucks, Lancaster, and Chester. The refugees, however, were not without friends. To several Quakers they were indebted for many acts of kindness and generosity.

Among those deported to Philadelphia was one of the Le Blanc family, a boy of seventeen, Charles Le Blanc. Early in life he engaged in commerce, and in the course of a long and successful career in Philadelphia amassed an enormous fortune, including large estates in the colonies and in Canada. After his death in 1816 there were many claimants to his estate, and the litigation over it is not yet ended.

The Acadians taken to New York were evidently as poor as their fellow-refugees at Philadelphia. An Act of July 6, 1756, recites that 'a certain number have been received into this

---

[83] Jonathan Belcher, governor of New Jersey and later of Massachusetts. He was the father of the chief justice of Nova Scotia.

colony, poor, naked, and destitute of every convenience and support of life, and, to the end that they may not continue as they now really are, useless to His Majesty, to themselves, and a burthen to this colony, be it enacted...that the Justices of the Peace...be required and empowered to bind with respectable families such as are not arrived at the age of twenty-one years, for such a space of time as they may think proper.' The justices were to make the most favourable contracts for them, and when their term of service expired, they were to be paid either in implements of trade, clothing, or other gratuity.

In the month of August 1756 one hundred and ten sturdy Acadian boys and girls made their appearance in New York. They had travelled all the way from Georgia in the hope of finding means to return to Acadia. Great was their disappointment when they were seized by the authorities and placed out to service. Later some of the parents straggled in, but they were dispersed immediately in Orange and Westchester counties, and some on Long Island, in charge of a constable. The New York Mercury of July 1757 reported that a number of the neutrals had been captured near Fort Edward while on their way to Crown Point. Between the arrival of the first detachment in New York and the month of August 1757 the colony was compelled to provide for large numbers who came in from distant places. To prevent any further escape the sheriffs were commanded to secure all the Acadians, except women and children, in the county gaol.

At a later date these unfortunates were put to a strange use. Sir Harry Moore, governor of the colony of New York (1765-69), had designs upon the French colony at Santo Domingo, in the West Indies, and desired plans of the town and its fortifications. So he entered into correspondence with the French Admiral, Count d'Estaing, offering to transport thither seventy Acadian families in order that they might live under the French flag. The count accepted the offer and issued a proclamation to the Acadians inviting them to Santo Domingo. Moore had arranged that John Hanson should conduct the exiles to their new home. Hanson, on arriving at the French colony, was to take a contract to build houses and make out the desired military plans while so engaged. He succeeded in transporting the Acadians, but failed in the real object of his mission. He was not allowed the liberty of building houses in Santo Domingo. The Acadians who went to the West Indies suffered greatly. The tropical climate proved disastrous to men and women who had been reared in the atmosphere of the Bay of Fundy. They crawled under trees and shrubs to escape the fierce rays of the sun. Numbers of them perished and life became a burden to the others.

Far different was the lot of the Acadians who were sent to Maryland.[84] arrived here the last of the vessels from Nova Scotia with French Neutrals for this place, which makes four within this fortnight bringing upwards of nine hundred of them. As the poor people have been deprived of their settlements in Nova Scotia, and sent here for some political reason bare and destitute, Christian charity, nay, common humanity, calls on every one according to his ability to lend assistance and to help these objects of compassion.'] There they were kindly received and found, no doubt, a happier lot than in any of the other colonies. Those landed at Baltimore were at first lodged in private houses and in a building belonging to a Mr Fotherall, where they had a little chapel. And it was not long before the frugal and industrious exiles were able to construct small but comfortable houses of their own on South Charles Street, giving to that quarter of the city the name of French Town. Many of them found employment on the waterside and in navigation. The old and infirm picked oakum.

Massachusetts at one time counted in the colony a thousand and forty of the exiles, but all these had not come direct on the ships from Nova Scotia. Many of them had wandered in from other colonies. The people of Massachusetts loved not Catholics and Frenchmen; nevertheless, in some instances they received the refugees with especial kindness. At Worcester a small tract of land was set aside for the Acadians to cultivate, with permission to hunt deer at all seasons. The able-bodied men and women toiled in the fields as reapers, and added to their income in the evening by making wooden

---

[84] The Maryland Gazette, Annapolis, December 4, 1755, said: 'Sunday last [November 30

implements. The Acadians were truly primitive in their methods. 'Although,' says a writer of the time, 'they tilled the soil they kept no animals for labour. The young men drew their material for fencing with thongs of sinew, and they turned the earth with a spade. The slightest allusion to their native land drew forth tears and many of the aged died of a broken heart.'

As French Neutrals began to come into Boston from other towns, the selectmen of that city protested vigorously and passed the people on to outlying parishes, promising, however, to be responsible for their maintenance should they become a public charge. Several instances are recorded of children being sent to join their parents. A certain number were confined in the workhouse and in the provincial hospital. But on December 6, 1760, the authorities gave instructions for the hospital to be cleared to make room for the colonial troops who were returning home, many of them suffering from contagious diseases; and the Acadians were forthwith turned out.

Although none of the Acadians appear to have been sent direct to Louisiana, large numbers of them found their way thither from various places, especially from Virginia, where they were not allowed to remain. Finding in Louisiana men speaking their own tongue, they felt a sense of security, and gradually settled down with a degree of contentment. There are to-day in various parishes of the state of Louisiana many thousand Acadian-Americans.

Of the Acadians who succeeded in escaping deportation and went into voluntary exile, many sought shelter in New Brunswick, on the rivers Petitcodiac, Memramcook, Buctouche, Richibucto, and Miramichi, and along Chaleur Bay. The largest of the settlements so formed was the one on the Miramichi, at Pierre Beaubair's seigneury, where the village of Nelson now stands. For several years these refugees in New Brunswick bravely struggled against hardship, disease, and starvation; but in the late autumn of 1759 the several settlements sent deputies to Colonel Frye at Fort Cumberland, asking on what terms they would be received back to Nova Scotia. Frye took a number of them into the fort for the winter, and presented their case to Lawrence. It was decided to accept their submission and supply them with provisions. But when the people returned they were held as vassals; and many of them afterwards were either sent out of the province to France or England, or left it voluntarily for St Pierre and Miquelon or the West Indies.

Other fugitives of 1755, fifteen hundred, according to one authority,[85] succeeded in reaching Quebec. Here their lot was a hard one. Bigot and his myrmidons plundered everybody, and the starving Acadians did not escape. They had managed to bring with them a little money and a few household treasures, of which they were soon robbed. For a time they were each allowed but four ounces of bread a day, and were reduced, it is said, to searching the gutters for food. To add to their miseries smallpox broke out among them and many perished from the disease. After Quebec surrendered and the victorious British army entered the gates, some two hundred of them, under the leadership of a priest, Father Coquart, who apparently had a passport from General Murray, marched through the wilderness to the headwaters of the St John and went down to Fort Frederick at the mouth of that river. Colonel Arbuthnot, the British commandant there, treated them generously. In 1761, however, many Acadians at the St John were seized and deported to Halifax, where they were held as prisoners of war, but were provided with rations and given 'good wages for road-making.'[86] Of those who escaped this deportation, some established themselves on the Kennebecasis river and some went up the St John to St Anne's, now Fredericton. But even here the Acadians were not to have a permanent home. Twenty years later, when the war of the Revolution ended and land was needed for the king's disbanded soldiers, the lands of the Acadians were seized. Once more the unfortunate people sought new homes, and found them at last along the banks of Chaleur Bay and of the Madawaska, where thousands of their descendants now rudely cultivate the fields and live happy, contented lives.

The deportation did not bring peace to Nova Scotia. Acadians of New Brunswick and of those who had sought

---

[85] Placide Gaudet, 'Acadian Genealogy and Notes,' Canadian Archives Report, 1905. vol. ii, part iii, Appendix A, p. xv.
[86] MacMechan in Canada and its Provinces, vol. xiii, p. 115.

refuge in the forest fastnesses of the peninsula and Cape Breton joined with the Indians in guerilla warfare against the British; and there was more killing of settlers and more destruction of property from Indian raids than ever before. Early in the month of January 1756 British rangers rounded up over two hundred Acadian prisoners at Annapolis, and put them on board a vessel bound for South Carolina. The prisoners, however, made themselves masters of the ship and sailed into the St John river in February. French privateers, manned by Acadians, haunted the Bay of Fundy and the Gulf of St Lawrence and carried off as prizes twelve British vessels. But in 1761 the British raided a settlement of the marauders on Chaleur Bay, and took three hundred and fifty prisoners to Halifax.

We have seen in a preceding chapter that from time to time numbers of Acadians voluntarily left their homes in Nova Scotia and went over to French soil. Many of these took up their abode in Ile St Jean at Port La Joie (Charlottetown), where they soon formed a prosperous settlement and were able to supply not only the fortress but the town of Louisbourg with provisions. Those who were not engaged in agricultural pursuits found profitable employment in the fisheries. There were also thriving settlements at Point Prince, St Peter, and Malpeque. It is computed that in 1755 there were at least four thousand Acadians in Ile St Jean. A much larger estimate is given by some historians. Now, on the fall of Louisbourg in 1758, some of the British transports which had brought out troops from Cork to Halifax were ordered to Ile St Jean to carry the Acadians and French to France. The largest of these transports was the Duke William; another was named the Violet. Some of the Acadians made good their escape, but many were dragged on board the vessels. On the Duke William was a missionary priest, and before the vessels sailed he was called upon to perform numerous marriages, for the single men had learned that if they landed unmarried in France they would be forced to perform military service, for which they had no inclination. Nine transports sailed in consort, but were soon caught in a violent tempest and scattered. On December 10 the Duke William came upon the Violet in a sinking condition; and notwithstanding all efforts at rescue, the Violet went down with nearly four hundred souls. Meanwhile the Duke William herself had sprung a leak. For a time she was kept afloat by empty casks in the hold, but presently it became evident that the ship was doomed. The long-boat was put out and filled to capacity. And scarcely had the boat cleared when an explosion occurred and the Duke William went down, taking three hundred persons to a watery grave. The longboat finally reached Penzance with twenty-seven of the castaways. The other vessels probably found some French port.[87]

In Nova Scotia the Acadians were sorely needed. Even their bitter enemy, Jonathan Belcher, now lieutenant-governor,[88] wrote on June 18, 1761: 'By representations made to me from the new settlements in this province, it appears extremely necessary that the inhabitants should be assisted by the Acadians in repairing the dykes for the preservation and recovery of the marsh lands, particularly as on the progress of this work, in which the Acadians are the most skilful people in the country, the support and subsistence of several hundred of the inhabitants will depend.'[89] It seemed almost impossible to induce settlers to come to the province; and those who did

---

[87] In 1763 there were 2,370 Acadians in the maritime towns of France and 866 at various English ports. Many of these returned later to the land of their birth. See Canadian Archives Report, 1905, vol. ii, Appendix G, pp. 148 and 157.

[88] He succeeded Lawrence, who died in October 1760. Two documents in the Colonial Office Records raise more than a suspicion that Lawrence had been by no means an exemplary public servant. The first is a complaint made by Robert Sanderson, speaker of the first legislature of Nova Scotia, elected in 1758, respecting the grave misconduct of Lawrence in many stated particulars, including the release from gaol before trial of prisoners charged with burglary and other grave offences as well as the misapplication of public funds. The second is a letter from the Lords of Trade to Belcher laying down rules for his conduct as lieutenant-governor and referring to the many serious charges against his predecessor, some of which they regard as having substantial foundation, and none of which they express themselves as altogether rejecting. Consult, in the Public Archives, Canada, Nova Scotia A, vol. lxv.

[89] Nova Scotia Documents, p. 319.

come seem to have been unable to follow the example of the former owners of the soil, for much of the land which had been reclaimed from the sea by the labour and ingenuity of the Acadian farmers was once more being swept by the ocean tides.

Yet, when the Acadians began to return to Nova Scotia in ever-increasing numbers, Belcher and the Halifax Council decided to banish them again. In 1762 five transports loaded with prisoners were sent to Massachusetts, but that colony wanted no more Acadians and sent them back. Belcher had some difficulty in explaining his action to the home government. And the Lords of Trade did not scruple to censure him.

When the Treaty of Paris (February 1763) brought peace between France and England and put an end to French power in America, the Acadians could no longer be considered a menace, and there was no good political reason for keeping them out of Canada or Nova Scotia. Almost immediately those in exile began to seek new homes among people of their own race and religion. The first migration seems to have been from New England by the Lake Champlain route to the province of Quebec. There they settled at various places, notably L'Acadie, St Gregoire, Nicolet, Becancour, St Jacques-l'Achigan, St Philippe, and Laprairie. In these communities hundreds of their descendants still live.

In 1766 the exiles in Massachusetts assembled in Boston and decided to return to their native land. All who were fit to travel, numbering about nine hundred men, women, and children, marched through the wilderness along the Atlantic coast and across New Brunswick to the isthmus of Chignecto. Many perished by the way, overcome by the burden and fatigue of a journey which lasted over four months. But at last the weary pilgrims approached their destination. And near the site of the present village of Coverdale in Albert county, New Brunswick, they were attracted to a small farmhouse by the crowing of a cock in the early dawn. To their unspeakable joy they found the house inhabited by a family of their own race. Here they halted for a few days, making inquiry concerning their old friends. Then they tramped on in different directions. Everywhere on the isthmus the scene was changed. The old familiar farm buildings had disappeared or were occupied by strangers of an alien tongue, and even the names of places were known no more. Some journeyed to Windsor and some to Annapolis, where they remained for a time. At length, on the western shores of the present counties of Digby and Yarmouth, they found a home, and there to-day live the descendants of these pilgrims. For miles their neat villages skirt the shores of the ocean and the banks of the streams. For a century and a half they have lived in peace, cultivating their salt-marsh lands and fresh-water meadows, preserving the simple manners, customs, and language of their ancestors. They form a community apart, a hermit community. But they are useful citizens, good farmers, hardy fishermen and sailors.

Both in Canada and in the United States are to be found many Acadians occupying exalted positions. The chief justice of the Supreme Court of Louisiana, Joseph A. Breaux, is of Acadian descent. In Canada the Rt Rev. Edward Le Blanc, bishop of Acadia, the Hon. P. E. Le Blanc, lieutenant-governor of the province of Quebec, and the Hon. Pascal Poirier, senator, are Acadians, as are many other prominent men. And Isabella Labarre, who married Jean Foret, of Beaubassin, was one of the maternal ancestors of Sir Wilfrid Laurier.

Save in the Maritime Provinces, it is not possible to count the offspring of the original French settlers of Acadia who came out from France in the seventeenth century. It is estimated that there were at the time of the expulsion ten or eleven thousand under the British flag, and four or five thousand in Ile St Jean and elsewhere on French territory. About six thousand were deported, as we have seen, and scattered over the British colonies. Undoubtedly a great number of Americans of to-day are descendants of those exiles, but, except at the mouth of the Mississippi, they are merged in the general population and their identity is lost. Neither can we tell how many of those who found their way to Old France remained there permanently. For upwards of twenty years the French government was concerned in finding places for them. Some were settled on estates; some were sent to Corsica; others, as late as 1778, went to Louisiana. Nor can we estimate the number of Acadians in the province of Quebec, for no distinction has been made between them and the general French-Canadian population. For the Maritime Provinces, however, we have the count of the census of 1911. This shows 98,611 in New Brunswick, 51,746 in Nova Scotia, and 13,117 in Prince Edward Island, a total of 163,474 in the three provinces. The largest communities are those of Gloucester, Victoria, Madawaska, and Kent counties in New Brunswick, and of Digby and Yarmouth in Nova Scotia. Several thousand Acadians are counted in Cape Breton; so, too, in Halifax and Cumberland counties. But in the county of Annapolis, where stands the site of the first settlement formed on the soil of Canada—the site of the ancient stronghold of Acadia—and which for many generations was the principal home of the Acadian people, only two or three hundred Acadians are to be found to-day; while, looking out over Minas Basin, the scene of so much sorrow and suffering, one solitary family keeps its lonely vigil in the village of Grand Pre.

BIBLIOGRAPHICAL NOTE

The story of Acadia and the Acadians has been told many times, but most of the treatises on the subject are unsatisfactory from the historical point of view, either because of the biased attitude taken by the authors or because of their inadequate use of original sources. The present writer has deliberately avoided consulting secondary works. The following titles, however, are here suggested for the benefit of the reader who wishes to become acquainted with the literature of the subject.

Thomas Chandler Haliburton, 'An Historical and Statistical Account of Nova Scotia' (2 vols., Halifax, 1829), the earliest general history of the province, based on but slight knowledge of the sources. Beamish Murdoch, 'A History of Nova Scotia' (3 vols., Halifax, 1865-1867), fuller and more accurate than Haliburton, but having less charm of style. Francis Parkman, 'France and England in North America' (9 vols., Boston, 1865-1892, and later editions). The chapters on Acadia are scattered through several volumes of this valuable series: see the volumes entitled 'Pioneers of France, The Old Regime, A Half-Century of Conflict', and 'Montcalm and Wolfe'. Celestin Moreau, 'Histoire de l'Acadie Francoise' (Paris, 1873). James Hannay, 'History of Acadia' (St John, 1879). P. H. Smith, 'Acadia: A Lost Chapter in American History' (Pawling, N.Y., 1884). Justin Winsor, 'Narrative and Critical History of America': see vols. iv and v (Boston, 1884, 1887), containing scholarly bibliographical notes. Abbe H. R. Casgrain, 'Un Pelerinage au pays d'Evangeline' (Quebec, 1887). Rameau de Saint-Pere, 'Une Colonie Feodale en Amerique, l'Acadie' (2 vols., Paris and Montreal, 1889): the appendix contains some interesting documents. Edouard Richard, 'Acadia: Missing Links of a Lost Chapter in American History' (2 vols., New York and Montreal, 1895). Rev. Wm. O. Raymond, 'The River St John' (2nd ed., St John, 1910).

Some older works which incidentally contain interesting or valuable references to Acadia may be mentioned. F. X. Charlevoix, 'Histoire et Description Generale de la Nouvelle France' (3 vols., Paris, 1744; and translation by J. G. Shea, 6 vols., New York, 1866-1872). Abbe Guillaume Thomas Raynal,

'Histoire philosophique et politique des Etablissemens dans les deux Indes' (5 vols., Paris, 1770), which first painted a picture of an idyllic life of simplicity and happiness among the Acadians. Thomas Hutchinson, 'History of the Colony of Massachusetts Bay' (3 vols., London, 1765-1828). G. R. Minot, 'Continuation of the History of the Province of Massachusetts Bay' (2 vols., Boston, 1798-1803). Jeremy Belknap, 'History of New Hampshire' (3 vols., Boston, 1791-1792). W. D. Williamson, 'History of the State of Maine' (2 vols., Hallowell, 1832). The last four works are of much value for the relations between Acadia and the New England colonies.

Among special studies of note are: J. G. Kohl, 'Discovery of Maine' ('Documentary History of the State of Maine,' vol. i, 1869). H. P. Biggar, 'Early Trading Companies of New France' (Toronto, 1901). Henry Kirke, 'The First English Conquest of Canada' (London, 1871; 2nd ed., 1908), a work which devotes much space to the early establishments in Nova Scotia. Rev. Edmund F. Slafter, 'Sir William Alexander and American Colonization' (Boston, 1873), which contains a valuable selection of documents. Abbe J. A. Maurault, 'Histoire des Abenakis' (Sorel, 1866). Pascal Poirier, 'Origine des Acadiens' (Montreal, 1874) and 'Des Acadiens deportes a Boston en 1755' ('Trans. Roy. Soc. of Can.,' 3rd series, vol. ii, 1908).

Several local histories contain information regarding the Acadian exiles in the American colonies. William Lincoln, 'History of Worcester, Massachusetts' (Worcester, 1862). Bernard C. Steiner, 'History of the Plantation of Menunkatuck and of the Original Town of Guilford, Connecticut' (Baltimore, 1897). Rev. D. P. O'Neill, 'History of St Raymond's Church, Westchester New York.' J. T. Scharf, 'Chronicles of Baltimore' (Baltimore, 1874). Edward M'Crady, 'History of South Carolina under the Royal Government, 1719-1776' (New York, 1899).

Of original sources, many of the more important narratives are available in print. Champlain's Voyages, a work which appeared in its first form in 1604: recent editions are by Laverdiere (6 vols., Quebec, 1870); translation by Slafter (3 vols., The Prince Society, Boston, 1880-1882); and translations of portions by W. L. Grant in Jameson's 'Original Narratives of Early American History' (New York, 1907). Marc Lescarbot,

'Histoire de la Nouvelle France' (1st ed., Paris, 1609): a new edition with translation has been edited by W. L. Grant (The Champlain Society, 3 vols., Toronto, 1907-1914). Nicolas Denys, 'Description Geographique et Historique des Costes de l'Amerique Septentrionale' (Paris, 1672): new edition and translation by William F. Ganong (The Champlain Society, Toronto, 1908). Denys tells of De Monts, Poutrincourt, Biencourt, and the La Tours.

Supplementary information can be obtained from 'The Jesuit Relations' (the first number, by Father Biard, was published at Lyons, 1616); see edition with translation, by R. G. Thwaites (Cleveland, 1896). See also Purchas, 'His Pilgrimes,' vol. iv (1625); and John Winthrop, 'History of New England,' edited by James Savage (2 vols., Boston, 1825-1826), and by J. K. Hosmer in 'Original Narratives of Early American History' (New York, 1908). Gaston du Boscq de Beaumont, 'Les Derniers Jours de l'Acadie,' 1748-1758 (Paris, 1899) contains many interesting letters and memoirs from the French side at the time of the expulsion.

There are several important collections of documentary sources available in print. The 'Memorials of the English and French Commissaries concerning the Limits of Nova Scotia or Acadia' (London and Paris, 1755) contains the arguments and documents produced on both sides in the dispute regarding the Acadian boundaries. Many documents of general interest are to be found in the 'Collection de Documents relatifs a l'Histoire de la Nouvelle France' (4 vols., Quebec, 1885); in 'Documents relative to the Colonial History of the State of New York,' edited by O'Callaghan and Fernow (15 vols., Albany, 1856-1887), particularly vol. ix; and in the 'Collections' of the Massachusetts Historical Society (Boston, 1792-). The 'Collections' of the Nova Scotia Historical Society (Halifax, 1879-), besides modern studies, contain many valuable contemporary documents, including 'Journal of Colonel Nicholson at the Capture of Annapolis,' 'Diary of John Thomas,' and 'Journal of Colonel John Winslow.' Thomas and Winslow are among the most important sources for the expulsion.

The 'Report on Canadian Archives' for 1912 prints several interesting documents bearing on the early history of Acadia, and the Report for 1905 (vol. ii) contains documents relating to the expulsion, edited by Placide Gaudet. The calendars contained in various Reports to which references are made below may also be consulted. The British Government publications, the 'Calendar of State Papers, Colonial Series, America and West Indies,' which has been brought down only to 1702, and the 'Acts of the Privy Council, Colonial Series,' are also useful. But perhaps the most valuable of all is the volume entitled 'Selections from the Public Documents of the Province of Nova Scotia,' edited by Thomas B. Akins (Halifax, 1869), though the editor has taken many liberties with his texts. A volume entitled 'Nova Scotia Archives II,' edited by Archibald MacMechan (Halifax, 1900), contains calendars of Governors' Letter Books and a Commission Book, 1713-1741.

The principal manuscript collections of material for Acadian history are in Paris, London, Boston, Halifax, and Ottawa. In Paris are the official records of French rule in America. Of the 'Archives des Colonies,' deposited at the 'Archives Nationales,' the following series are most important:

Series B: Letter Books of Orders of the King and Dispatches from 1663 onward (partially calendared in Canadian Archives 'Reports' for 1899; Supplement, 1904 and 1905).

Series C: correspondence received from the colonies, which is subdivided geographically. All the American colonies have letters relating to the refugee Acadians, but the most important section for general Acadian history is C-11, which relates to Canada and its dependencies, including Acadia itself, Ile Royale, now Cape Breton, and Ile St Jean, now Prince Edward Island.

Series F, which includes in its subdivisions documents relating to commercial companies and religious missions, and the Moreau St Mery Collection of miscellaneous official documents.

Series G: registers, censuses, lists of Acadian refugees, and notarial records.

The 'Ministere des Affaires Etrangeres' has, in the 'Angleterre' section of its 'Correspondence Politique' and the 'Amerique' section of its 'Memoires et Documents,' extensive material on the disputes with the English Government over Acadia. The 'Archives de la Marine' (Series B), which is divided into eight sub-series, has a vast collection of documents relating to America, including Acadia. Acadian material is also found scattered through other series of the 'Archives Nationales' and among the manuscripts of the 'Bibliotheque Nationale.' At the town of Vire, in France, among the municipal archives, are to be found the papers of Thomas Pichon, a French officer at Louisbourg and Beausejour, who after the fall of Beausejour lived on intimate terms with the British in Nova Scotia.

In London most of the official documents for the period under consideration in this volume are preserved in the Public Record Office. The most useful collections are among the Colonial Office Papers: Series C.O. 5, formerly described as America and West Indies, embraces the papers of the office of the Secretary of State who had charge of the American colonies; and C.O. 217-221, formerly, for the most part, described as Board of Trade Nova Scotia, contains the correspondence of the Board of Trade relating to Nova Scotia. The 'Admiralty Papers and Treasury Board Papers' likewise contain considerable material for the story of British administration in Acadia.

In the British Museum are some manuscripts of interest, the most noteworthy being Lieutenant-Governor Vetch's Letter Book (Sloane MS. 3607), and the Brown Collection (Additional MSS. 190694). These are papers relating to Nova Scotia and the Acadians, 1711-1794, including the correspondence of Paul Mascarene.

In Boston two important collections are to be found: the Massachusetts State Archives, which contain some original documents bearing on the relations between New England and Nova Scotia, and others connected with the disposal of those Acadians who were transported to Massachusetts, and many transcripts made from the French Archives; and the Parkman Papers, which are now in the possession of the Massachusetts Historical Society.

The Public Records of Nova Scotia at Halifax contain transcripts from the Paris and Massachusetts Archives relating to Acadia, transcripts from the Public Record Office at London and from the British Museum, letter-books of the Governors of Nova Scotia, minutes of the Executive Council, and much miscellaneous correspondence and papers belonging to our period.

In the Public Archives of Canada at Ottawa a very extensive collection of transcripts has been assembled comprising all the more important official documents relating to Acadia. A full description of most of the series can be obtained from David W. Parker's 'Guide to the Documents in the Manuscript Room at the Public Archives of Canada,' vol. i (Ottawa, 1914). The series known as Nova Scotia State Papers is divided into several sub-series: A. Correspondence from 1603 onwards, made up chiefly of transcripts from the Papers of the Secretary of State and of the Board of Trade at the Public Record Office, but including some from the British Museum and elsewhere (a calendar is to be found in the 'Report on Canadian Archives' for 1894); B. Minutes of the Executive Council of Nova Scotia, 1720-1785; E. Instructions to Governors, 1708 onwards. The Archives also possess transcripts of the French 'Archives des Colonies,' Series B, down to 1746, Series C-11 and parts of Series F and G, and of many documents of the 'Ministere des Affaires Etrangeres,' of the 'Archives de la Marine,' Series B, and of the 'Bibliotheque Nationale' (among the latter being the 'Memoire instructif de la conduite du Sr. de la Tour'). Also transcripts of the Pichon Papers, of much of the C.O. 5 Series for this period in the Public Record Office, London; of Vetch's Letter Book, the Brown Collection and other sources in the British Museum; and of parts of the Parkman Papers, and other records regarding the exiled Acadians in the Massachusetts Archives.